PENGUIN  CLASSICS

ALL MY SONS

ARTHUR MILLER was born in New York City in 1915 and studied at the University of Michigan. His plays include *All My Sons* (1947), *Death of a Salesman* (1949), *The Crucible* (1953), *A View from the Bridge* and *A Memory of Two Mondays* (1955), *After the Fall* (1964), *Incident at Vichy* (1965), *The Price* (1968), *The Creation of the World and Other Business* (1972), and *The American Clock* (1980). He has also written two novels, *Focus* (1945) and *The Misfits*, which was filmed in 1960, and the text for *In Russia* (1969), *In the Country* (1977), and *Chinese Encounters* (1979), three books of photographs by Inge Morath. His most recent works include a memoir, *Timebends* (1987), the plays *The Ride Down Mt. Morgan* (1991), *The Last Yankee* (1993), *Broken Glass* (1994), and *Mr. Peters' Connections* (1999), *Echoes Down the Corridor: Collected Essays, 1944–2000*, and *On Politics and the Art of Acting* (2001). He has twice won the New York Drama Critics Circle Award, and in 1949 he was awarded the Pulitzer Prize. He was the recipient of the National Book Foundation 2001 Medal for Distinguished Contribution to American Letters, he was awarded with the prize Prince of Asturias of Letters in 2002, and most recently in 2003 was awarded the Jerusalem Prize.

CHRISTOPHER BIGSBY has published more than twenty-five books on British and American culture. His works include studies of African American writing, American theater, English drama, and popular culture. He is the author of three novels, *Hester*, *Pearl*, and *Still Lives*, and he has written plays for radio and television. He is also a regular broadcaster for the BBC. He is currently professor of American Studies at the University of East Anglia, in Norwich, England.

BY ARTHUR MILLER

DRAMA
The Golden Years
The Man Who Had All the Luck
All My Sons
Death of a Salesman
An Enemy of the People (*adaptation of the play by Ibsen*)
The Crucible
A View from the Bridge
After the Fall
Incident at Vichy
The Price
The American Clock
The Creation of the World and Other Business
The Archbishop's Ceiling
The Ride Down Mt. Morgan
Broken Glass
Mr. Peters' Connections

ONE-ACT PLAYS
A View from the Bridge, *one-act version, with* A Memory of Two Mondays
Elegy for a Lady (*in* Two-Way Mirror)
Some Kind of Love Story (*in* Two-Way Mirror)
I Can't Remember Anything (*in* Danger: Memory!)
Clara (*in* Danger; Memory!)
The Last Yankee

OTHER WORKS
Situation Normal
The Misfits (*a cinema novel*)
Focus (*a novel*)
I Don't Need You Anymore (*short stories*)
In the Country (*reportage with Ingc Morath photographs*)
Chinese Encounters (*reportage with Inge Morath photographs*)
In Russia (*reportage with Inge Morath photographs*)
Salesman in Beijing (*a memoir*)
Timebends (*autobiography*)
Homely Girl, A Life (*novella*)
On Politics and the Art of Acting

COLLECTIONS
Arthur Miller's Collected Plays (Volumes I and II)
The Portable Arthur Miller
The Theater Essays of Arthur Miller (*Robert Martin, editor*)
Echoes Down the Corridor: Collected Essays, 1944–2000

VIKING CRITICAL LIBRARY EDITIONS
Death of a Salesman (*edited by Gerald Weales*)
The Crucible (*edited by Gerald Weales*)

TELEVISION WORKS
Playing for Time

SCREENPLAYS
The Misfits
Everybody Wins
The Crucible

ARTHUR MILLER

All My Sons

A DRAMA IN THREE ACTS

With an Introduction by
CHRISTOPHER BIGSBY

PENGUIN BOOKS

PENGUIN BOOKS

Published by the Penguin Group

Penguin Group (USA) Inc., 375 Hudson Street, New York, New York 10014, U.S.A.
Penguin Group (Canada), 90 Eglinton Avenue East, Suite 700, Toronto,
Ontario, Canada M4P 2Y3 (a division of Pearson Penguin Canada Inc.)
Penguin Books Ltd, 80 Strand, London WC2R 0RL, England
Penguin Ireland, 25 St Stephen's Green, Dublin 2, Ireland (a division of Penguin Books Ltd)
Penguin Group (Australia), 250 Camberwell Road, Camberwell,
Victoria 3124, Australia (a division of Pearson Australia Group Pty Ltd)
Penguin Books India Pvt Ltd, 11 Community Centre, Panchsheel Park,
New Delhi – 110 017, India
Penguin Group (NZ), 67 Apollo Drive, Rosedale, North Shore 0632, New Zealand
(a division of Pearson New Zealand Ltd)
Penguin Books (South Africa) (Pty) Ltd, 24 Sturdee Avenue, Rosebank,
Johannesburg 2196, South Africa

Penguin Books Ltd, Registered Offices: 80 Strand, London WC2R 0RL, England

First Published in the United States of America by Reynal & Hitchcock 1947
This edition with an introduction by Christopher Bigsby
published in Penguin Books 2000

45 47 49 50 48 46 44

LIBRARY OF CONGRESS CATALOGING IN PUBLICATION DATA
Miller, Arthur, 1915–
All my sons: a drama in three acts / Arthur Miller; edited and with an introduction by
Christopher Bigsby.
p. cm.
ISBN 978-0-14-118546-0
1. World War, 1939–1945—United States—Drama.   2. Aircraft industry—Corrupt
practices—Drama.   3. Aircraft industry—Miliatary aspects—Drama.   4. Fathers and
sons—Drama.   I. Bigsby, C. W. E.   II. Title.
PS3525.I5156 A7   2000
812'.52—dc21   00–032621

Printed in the United States of America
Set in Bembo
Designed by Sabrina Bowers

CONTENTS

INTRODUCTION

WHEN ARTHUR MILLER began writing *All My Sons* in 1945, he was thirty years old. The author of a number of radio plays and the screenplay for a film—*The Story of GI Joe*—he was nonetheless finding theater a more difficult proposition. After a successful college career, he had written a play for the Federal Theater, only to see that organization closed down by Congress. His only professionally produced work, *The Man Who Had All the Luck* (1944), had failed after a matter of days. By contrast, his first novel, *Focus* (1945), was a considerable success, suggesting that he might be better employed as a writer of fiction. He determined, though, to make one more assault on the theater.

He first heard the story on which he would base *All My Sons* from his mother-in-law in Ohio. She had read of a young woman who informed on her father. He had been defrauding the military. In the context of Miller's later career—his resistance to informing before the House Un-American Activities Committee, and his portrait of informers in *The Crucible* and *A View from the Bridge*—it is fascinating to think what he might have made of such an act, but this element swiftly disappeared. The young woman became a man, "because I didn't know much about girls then,"[1] and a new family context was created. Until that point, Miller had rarely spent more than three months on a play. This new one took two and a half years to write.

Begun in wartime but produced in peacetime, it lost something of the air of scandal that might have accompanied an earlier production and became, in essence, what it had always been in his own mind: a study of denial, of guilt, of social responsibility. It is a play in which past and present are brought together out of a belief in causality, a conviction that personal meaning and identity are the product of willed actions.

All My Sons concerns a manufacturer of aircraft parts, Joe Keller, who under the pressure of wartime production allows a batch of faulty cylinder heads to be supplied to the Army Air Force, knowing that they may cause catastrophic failure and thus endanger life. He does so rather than risk losing the contract and possibly his business, which he wishes to pass on to his sons. In the subsequent court case he denies responsibility, allowing his employee and neighbor, Steve Deever, to take the blame. Deever's daughter, Ann, meanwhile, is engaged to Keller's son Larry. Following their father's conviction both she and her brother, George, sever all connection with him, refusing to visit him in prison or even write to him. To sustain his own family, Keller, it seems, sacrifices another and, beyond that, a wider family, those who die as a result of his actions.

When Larry, a pilot, goes missing in action, Kate Keller refuses to acknowledge his death, not least because to do so would be to accept a connection between her husband's action and her own loss. The play opens as the Kellers' other son, Chris, invites Ann to stay, intending to propose a marriage which will, effectively, signify public acknowledgment of Larry's death and thus precipitate a crisis for all of them as past and present are brought into immediate confrontation. The action takes place in less than twenty-four hours.

Miller's failure to secure a production for his Federal Theater play, a densely poetic drama about Montezuma and Cortés called *The Golden Years*, together with the failed production of *The Man Who Had All the Luck*, whose style eluded director, critics, and audience alike (though both plays would be produced successfully fifty years later), led him to attempt a more recognizable form. To that end, he turned to Henrik Ibsen as a model. As he explained, he was drawn to Ibsen because in Ibsen's work the "enormous past was always heavily documented to the end that the present be comprehended with wholeness, as a moment in the flow of time," so that "it presents barely and unadorned what I believe is the biggest single dramatic problem, namely, how to dramatize what has gone before."[2]

Kate Keller, half desperately moved, half terrified, announces, "Everything that happened seems to be coming back."[3] So it does. That, indeed, is the circumstance of the play and its dialectic as the present interrogates the past and the past infiltrates the present. As Miller puts it, the chickens come home to roost.

At the beginning of the play Miller set himself to create an atmosphere of what he called "undisturbed normality."[4] The first act moves at a steady pace. It takes place "beneath a clear landscape in the broad light of a peaceful day."[5] However, as he remarked of Mordecai Gorelick's designedly ordinary setting, this only "made the deepening threat of the remainder more frightening,"[6] for into this recognizable domesticity, this Andrew Wyeth scene of a Sunday morning in an Ohio town, he gradually inserts corrosive elements. The night before, we soon learn, there was a storm. A tree has blown down, a tree planted to commemorate a life. More is to follow, in an elemental drama in which father destroys son and son destroys father.

It is high summer, the apogee of the year. Ahead lies the fall. In the garden, already, are plants "whose season is gone." The stump of the apple tree stands downstage, its upper trunk, branches still covered with fruit, lying beside it. Having said that he wished to be "as untheatrical as possible," and in particular wanting to ensure that "any metaphor, any image, any figure of speech . . . was removed if it even so slightly brought to consciousness the hand of the writer,"[7] he placed this tree at the heart not only of the stage but of the play, quite as much as Chekhov did the cherry orchard. Fallen in its prime, it undeniably stands as a correlative for a son apparently cut down in the war, and it is identified as such by the characters. A storm occurring on the eve of a family crisis might seem an unnecessary underscoring of a drama which has its own logic, its own emotional tone, its own internal dynamics. That it does not seem unduly theatrical is precisely because the symbolism is read into it by characters themselves neurotically alert to threat and vigilant for evidence of change. And change is about to come over the Keller household, though for the moment these people seem frozen in time.

There is no past that can be confronted with total honesty and no future that does not carry a threat as well as a promise; and the present is no more than a temporary condition. The characters inhabit a no-man's-land. The primary action driving the play has already occurred and been buried, apparently, beneath the routines of daily existence. The living are haunted by the dead, whom they seek to exorcise with a simple denial of reality. No action that any of the characters can take will alter what has happened. At stake, though, are truth, responsibility, and what Miller has called the evil of "unrelatedness." For in a play in which the principal characters are drawn together by family affiliation, it is the fractures in relationships that most concern him, the limitations of responsibility. The structure of the play, he insisted, was "to bring a man into the direct path of the consequences he has wrought."[8]

Joe Keller's crime is that he has sent defective cylinder heads for use in aircraft engines, has committed perjury, and has allowed others to bear responsibility rather than accept the consequences of his own actions. But this is not primarily a play about a crime. It is about a man's failure to understand the terms of the social contract. In Miller's wartime play *The Half-Bridge,* never produced, the ultimate crime, in a drama about espionage and blackmail, is not those breaches of the criminal law but the removal of the buoys which mark a safe passage through ocean waters. Remove such buoys, literal and symbolic, and there is no longer a common world from which we may derive either personal identity or social meaning. This is what is at stake in *All My Sons*—and not for Joe

Keller alone, since this is a play in which few if any of the characters could be said to be free of a self-concern that here, and else-
where in Miller's work, is the primary root of denial and betrayal
on a private and a social level.

When Ibsen discussed the first production of *The Wild Duck*
(clearly an influence on *All My Sons*) with the director of the
Christiana Theater, he stressed the "naturalness and realism" of the
play, at the heart of which, nonetheless, was an affecting symbol;
he also stressed the need for lighting that would reflect the "basic
mood" of each act.[9] Miller's play reveals a similar commitment to
realism and a similar symbol, though not with the same centrality
and force as the wild duck in the earlier work. Miller also, perhaps, learned from Ibsen about lighting that would reflect a mood.
In the first act the sun shines brightly, as Chris Keller and Ann
plan their wedding. In the second act it is twilight, as the mood
darkens. In the third, it is two o'clock in the morning, with the
moon casting a "bluish light" on people whose lives have been
drained, suddenly, of color and purpose alike.

The Keller home is hedged in by poplar trees and has a
"secluded atmosphere"; this physical description develops a meta-
phoric force as the play unfolds and we learn of the moral isolation
of this family, or at least of its patriarch. Miller pointedly tells us
the financial value of the seven-room family home (fifteen thousand dollars when it was built in the 1920s), not only as a note to
the director and designer but also as a clue to the actors, for whom
this is to be a house in which money has been a determinant
and "family" a defining term. Indeed, the word "money" recurs
throughout the play, as a kind of counterpoint to the idealism
generated by the war. Character after character invokes money as
a reason for relinquishing ideals or hopes. A next-door neighbor, a
doctor, has abandoned medical research, at his wife's insistence,
for a more lucrative general practice—"You wanted money, so I
made money" (76). Another neighbor becomes financially secure
because he has never served in the war. Joe Keller, whose wife

also stresses money, complains that his son Chris "don't understand money"; and Keller finally defends his own actions as no more than a reflection of a general morality: "Did they ship a gun or a truck outa Detroit before they got their price? Is that clean? It's dollars and cents, nickels and dimes; war and peace, it's nickels and dimes" (82).

Joe Keller is described as a "heavy man of stolid mind and build," a businessman who bears the imprint of "the machine worker and the boss"; "when he reads, when he speaks, when he listens, it is with the terrible concentration of the uneducated man for whom there is still wonder in many commonly known things, a man whose judgment must be dredged out of experience and a peasant-like common sense" (5–6). His life is a triumph over such disadvantages, a triumph he will not readily allow to slip between his fingers. He is a man for whom survival is a primary necessity. Having lived through the Depression, he knows how fragile a grasp he, or anyone, has on the world. Nor is survival only a matter of maintaining a way of life and a way of being. Keller survives by insulating himself from knowledge of the consequences of his actions, by denying involvement in the world.

Miller is not concerned simply with an individual whose values are at odds with those of his society. On the contrary, Joe Keller is not aberrant, except in the extremity of his crime. He represents a pragmatism that coexisted with the language and fact of idealism in wartime America. As Miller insisted, when he wrote the play, "everybody knew that a lot of hanky-panky was going on. . . . A lot of illicit fortunes were being made, a lot of junk was being sold to the armed services, we all knew that. The average person was violating rationing. All the rules were being violated every day but you wanted not to mention it."[10]

Indeed, as Miller observed in his introduction to the *Collected Plays*, *All My Sons* was conceived when the contrast between sacrifice and aggrandizement seemed both sharp and profoundly disturbing: "When all public voices were announcing the arrival of that great day when industry and labor were one, my personal experience was daily demonstrating that beneath the slogans nothing had changed." The play was thus "an unveiling of what I believed everybody knew but nobody publicly said."[11]

The play was finally produced after the war, in January 1947, but its themes transcended the immediate circumstances that had generated the story. Indeed, speaking in 1999, Miller still insisted on its continuing relevance, noting that audiences recognize the force, if not the justification, of Keller's defense of his actions, not least because they understand, while rejecting, his motives and acknowledge their own potential for complicity: "The justification that Joe Keller makes is that . . . you do what you have to do in order to survive," a defense which is "always understandable and always unacceptable." The fact is that audiences "know pretty well that given the kind of pressure that Joe Keller was under they might have collapsed too, so that people participate in the conflict. They don't stand apart entirely from it because they know they're vulnerable."[12]

When the play begins, Keller is seen reading the want ads in a Sunday newspaper. As he explains, he no longer reads the news section, in which, after all, he would have found his own name only a few years before. As his neighbor rightly remarks, "It's all bad news" (6). Joe and his wife live in fear of bad news, about their son and about the crime they have conspired to deny. Indeed, the son and the crime are braided together in their minds.

Keller is joined by two neighbors, one, Frank Lubey, "uncertain of himself . . . thirty-two and balding"; the other, Jim, a doctor, "wry, self-controlled . . . but with a wisp of sadness that clings to his self-effacing humor." Their wives are, respectively, Lydia, a "robust, laughing girl of twenty-seven," and Sue, "rounding forty, an overweight woman who fears it." These notes are for the actors, and there is more than a hint that this suburban setting contains elements of regret and anxiety which extend beyond the Kellers' backyard. The neighbors give something more than a social density to *All My Sons*; they are more than a chorus, refracting the views of the community. They contain in themselves the conflicts at the heart of the play, acknowledging, as they do, a tension between the pragmatic and the ideal, and recognizing the compromises that seem an inevitable aspect of daily living. Marriage itself, it seems—on the basis of the marriages in this play—offers an image of such compromises, a fact that will surely cast its shadow over the proposed relationship between Chris Keller and Ann Deever.

The play begins with Chris Keller's admission that he has invited his brother's fiancée, Ann, with the intention of proposing marriage to her. Since his mother still insists that Larry is alive, such an action must destroy her fragile faith, for the fact is that, rather than confront her with the truth, both husband and son have, until now, remained silent. However, when Chris says, "Being dishonest with her. That kind of thing always pays off" (15), this is a statement that foreshadows other forms of dishonesty and other prices that must be paid—as does Joe's reply, "I ignore what I gotta ignore" (16). Indeed, Chris himself, shortly thereafter, prevaricates in the face of his mother's questioning. And though the focus of the play seems to be on Joe, whose past failings are revealed and whose guilt is affirmed, an ambiguity attaches itself to Chris and becomes more profound as the play proceeds.

Chris's early statement, for example, that "I don't know why it is, but every time I reach out for something I want, I have to pull back because other people will suffer. My whole bloody life, time after time after time" (16), seems to lack substance, outside of the immediate issue of his proposed marriage. What, precisely, has he reached for that he has been denied or required to relinquish so that others would not suffer? Chris, we begin to realize, is a man who sees himself as a martyr, an idealist; yet the suspicion grows that this is an image behind which he hides. Doubts are swallowed up in this self-conscious presentation of himself as an honest man doing nothing more than demanding honesty, a self-denier only now able to assert his rights. He presents himself, to himself, as serving truth, but truth not only places him at risk; it becomes a means of directing attention away from himself and his own moral failings.

At the beginning of the play he announces, "I've been a good son too long, a good sucker. I'm through with it" (17). In what sense is this true, beyond his failure to confess his love to Ann for fear of disturbing his mother? He now declares his willingness to leave the family business if necessary, but in fact he is anxious to secure the terms on which he can remain, while condescending to it. The business, he explains to the father who has built it, as he knows, in part for him, doesn't "inspire" him. But what does? He speaks of having to "grub for money" (17), as he later speaks resentfully of having to join the "rat race." He wants, he explains, to build something he can give himself to, quite as though he were still pursuing his metaphor of immolation and sacrifice. Knowing that his father is desperate for him to stay, he threatens to leave. Marriage to Ann, he implies, will secure his loyalty to the business. She becomes his bargaining tool.

Chris feels guilty about his new happiness. In the war he led his men to their death. He is a survivor who feels the guilt of the survivor, a theme to which Miller would return in *After the Fall* (1964). Beyond that, he can see no connection between the sacrifices of war and the way of life it was supposedly fought to preserve, a bland materialism with no transcendence. Wartime camaraderie implies a concept of human relationships and a shared perception of worth that seems to have no correlative in a postwar world concerned with simple acquisitiveness. However, he seems quietly to abandon his own rhetoric: "Annie," he announces, "I'm going to make a fortune for you!" (36). It is a half-ironic remark that perhaps reflects something of his unacknowledged ambiguity as a participant in a tainted company.

Kate Keller, meanwhile, carries the authority in the house, defines its reality. In an earlier version of the text she was in an even more dominant position. Her faith in astrology—a faith that was designed to bolster her desperate belief in her son's survival—generated the play's original title: *The Sign of the Archer*. Astrology may, as Miller has suggested, have given way to psychology—his own flirting with mysticism revealing, he thought, one of the problems with his earlier plays, such as *The Golden Years* and *The Man Who Had All the Luck*, at least so far as Broadway was concerned—but Kate still remains a powerful figure. The relationship between father and son may move to the center of attention, but she holds a key to the action. It is her will that has sustained them and, in a sense, her desperate necessity that has infantilized them as she struggles to deny the truth, to reject causality. For her, nothing must change. The clock must be stopped. Chris must remain unmarried; her husband must remain a charming incompetent, unable to function in the simplest of matters—since to assume otherwise would be to accept a view of the world that could only destroy her.

If Joe Keller uses the family as a justification for his actions, it is equally vital to Kate because beyond it lies nothing but a kind of anarchy, exemplified by the death of a son. In that regard there is something of Steinbeck's Ma Joad about her; she is determined, until the very end, to maintain the integrity and reality of the family in the face of change and competing models of social responsibility. Indeed, *All My Sons*, with its emphasis on human solidarity, on the interests of mankind over those of the individual or the family group, clearly chimes with a central conviction of the 1930s, embodied in the work of Steinbeck, Odets, and even, in *To Have and Have Not* and *For Whom the Bell Tolls*, of Ernest Hemingway. "Marx said it. Abolish such families,"[13] remarks the protagonist of Odets's *Awake and Sing*.

Interestingly, Kate Keller is referred to as "Mother" not only by Chris and, not entirely incidentally, by her husband, but also by the playwright, her speeches being so indicated in the text. It suggests, perhaps, that Miller, whose stage directions describe her as "a woman of uncontrolled inspirations, and an overwhelming capacity for love" (18), feels close to her and alienated from her husband—who is the only other character in the play not referred to by his first name in the speech indicators. The fact is, however, that the power system in the family changed with Joe Keller's decision to send out the defective parts, and with the criminal case that followed. Kate's knowledge, at whatever level it operates within her, strips him of the authority he once wielded. He cedes his position as head of the house, living in a temporal void enforced by his wife. Her desperate need to deny the possibility of her son's death, understandable in its own terms, also derives from her desire to deny the connection between that death and her husband's actions.

That connection is there, long before Ann's revelation in Act III that the son deliberately took his own life, out of shame at his father's actions. It is a connection that Kate can continue to deny only so long as she can convince herself and others that he may have survived. If he has not survived, then such meaning as she has constructed for herself will dissolve. As she says, "If he's not coming back, then I'll kill myself" (22). Why? Not simply because she will be admitting the death, three years before, of a son—a terrible but hardly unique loss—but because a connection will be made between that death and the culpability she shares with her husband. In her mind, the only defense for Joe Keller's action is that it was done for the sake of their sons. If one son is not returning and the other may abandon them, then it stands stripped even of this justification. It must be named for what it is. As she says to her husband, "You above all have got to believe" (23). As a result, she keeps her son's memory polished, like the shoes she puts out ready for his return.

That connection, however, is readily made by Ann. Speaking of her father, whom she believes to be responsible for shipping the faulty parts, she says, "He knowingly shipped out parts that would crash an airplane. And how do we know Larry wasn't one of them?" When Keller shows signs of agitation at this suggestion, Kate interrupts to insist, "He's not dead, so there's no argument" (32).

Joe is an accommodationist. His public denials are matched by his private ones. When Kate asks if Chris has discussed marrying Ann, his reply is, "He didn't tell me any more than he told you" (21–22), though we have just witnessed such a discussion. Having practiced private deceit, he seems to have internalized his own denials. Urging Ann to persuade her father to return to the neighborhood after his imprisonment, he says, "Listen, you do like I did and you'll be all right" (30). The fact is that he is far from all right, but at this stage in the play we are in no position to know this, though already there are sufficient hints to undermine the assurance he displays.

He insists, apparently with conviction, that he himself deliberately chose to return and confront his skeptical neighbors: "None of them believed I was innocent. The story was, I pulled a fast one getting myself exonerated. . . . The beast! I was the beast; the guy who sold cracked cylinder heads to the Army Air Force; the guy who made twenty-one P-40s crash in Australia. . . . Except I wasn't, and there was a court paper in my pocket to prove I wasn't" (30).

Yet, of course, he was and knows he was. Is this, then, mere bravado—blatant, calculated lying—or has denial sunk so deep into his being that reality has been reinvented? The speech ends with his boast that fourteen months later he had "one of the best shops in the state again, a respected man again; bigger than ever" (30). Best. Bigger. The language of material success blots out the language of guilt. It is as though the words themselves define the real and are his defense against self-knowledge. In his own mind he stands doubly vindicated, by the court and by his renewed success.

The "only way you lick 'em is guts!" (30) he insists, though he has, of course, precisely lacked the courage to face the implications of his own actions. He believes, because he must believe, that there is a space between his actions and the self those actions define. His observation that "you play cards with a man you know he can't be a murderer" (31) is less a confident piece of advice than a desperate article of faith on the part of a man seeking confirmation that appearance finally matters more than reality.

His assurance, however, is easily deflated. A telephone call from Ann's brother, George, combined with her sudden appearance in the house, is enough to put him on the defensive: "She don't hold nothin' against me, does she? . . . I mean if she was sent here to find out something. . . . I mean if they want to open up the case again, for the nuisance value, to hurt us" (38). The call comes from Columbus, where Ann and George's father is in prison. Suddenly, and with no further prompting, Joe Keller insists that he wants a "clean start" for his son, that he wishes him to inherit what he built for him, "without shame." The very phrases imply an acknowledgment of the culpability he otherwise denies.

Already the questions begin to accumulate. Why this nervousness, why this insistence on a clean start and on being unashamed, if he is not guilty? And why does Miller indicate that Joe's son, too, responds "a little uneasily" to the inheritance he is offered, and that he is "a little frightened" when asked to affirm that there is nothing wrong with the money he receives from the company that will one day bear his name? As in Miller's later plays, the integrity of a name is of crucial importance to those who have conspired in subverting that integrity.

Ann's father has lost his name, his reputation, in the eyes of the community. Joe defends his own name and reputation by refusing to acknowledge the connection between himself and his actions, while his son tries to sustain his by asserting an idealism that is at odds with his equally evident self-interest. Ann Deever, meanwhile, is to change her name, becoming Ann Keller, a process that requires certain adjustments and accommodations on her part, her new identity implicating her in the moral values of the family she joins. The fact is that these are all characters whose motives are mixed, who contain contradictions and who display different levels of consciousness of that fact. They are all characters who insist on the integrity of their identity when they are in the process of denying it.

Miller has said that Joe Keller feels justified in his actions because if his business had been threatened he would have had nothing to hand on to his son and "that would be a fate worse than death because one of his psychological supports is that he is a provider . . . the father of the house . . . the man from whom all power and . . . energy flows." Nonetheless, "he does feel guilt about what he has done" while at the same time feeling that "there was no other way for him. . . . It's a crazy quilt of motivations and contradictions inside of him."[14] He would, Miller suggests, be a "sociopathic person" if he were wholly insensitive to the social rules he has broken, fully capable of suppressing guilt for his actions, yet at the same time he denies the force of his knowledge. His sensitivity is, hence, evidence both of his guilt and of the survival of a moral conscience.

Interestingly, Miller has also said that he does not see Keller as a criminal. Since Joe assuredly is a criminal—his culpability being slowly exposed—what Miller seems to mean is that he is not wholly so, that such a word hardly sums up a man who acknowledges a hierarchy of values in which the needs of the family are placed ahead of strangers with whom he feels no organic connection, a man whose denials seem necessary to his survival. But he is not the only person who survives by virtue of suppressing the truth.

Speaking of Kate, Rosemary Harris, who played the part in the London production, said: "One of the fascinating aspects of playing Kate is the question of how much she really knows or suspects. It is a very thin line."[15] Miller is more peremptory: "Kate knows everything from the time the curtain goes up . . . because she remembers the day it happened." On the other hand, "her life has consisted of trying to deny what she knows." The same is true of Chris, "but with him it is buried deeper because it is so intolerable—the idea of his betraying him and his comrades—that he simply will not consider it."[16]

There is, in other words, a layered consciousness in this supposedly realistic play, a sense that each character contains within himself or herself a debate about contending values, about competing versions of the moral world and of reality. The characters are drawn together by love, but that love becomes the source of a certain corruption. It is also not untinged with its opposite. When Chris precipitates the confrontation that is to destroy his father, Miller has said, he has "to feel a certain, almost vengeance upon his father or he would not be able to do what he does." It is he, more even than George Deever, who drives the issue to the point of crisis, and he who has "to feel resentment and hatred for his father, to some degree"[17] in order to do this.

Indeed, no one in this play is without culpability, without cruelty, without guilt. Kate's obsession with one son's fate makes her behave with a callous disregard for the future of the other. Ann and George act in some degree out of guilt for the cruelty with which they have treated their father. Even Joe Keller's suicide is, in part, an act of self-justification and "a counterblow to his wife and son." Reminding us that the Chinese reportedly hang themselves in the doorways of the people who have offended them, and that many suicides are motivated by a desire to accuse or leave a residue of guilt, Miller sees Joe as laying before his wife and son, the two people he had invoked as a justification for his actions, their own responsibility. Certainly Chris "would feel a burden of guilt to the end of his life, in part because . . . he really knew . . . that he should not have participated in the business without clearing this up earlier on."[18]

Joe Keller knows he is guilty but has to preserve the idea of his innocence. Kate knows, on some level, that her son is dead yet has to sustain the idea that he has survived, or deal not only with that calamity but also with the corrosive truth about her husband's actions. Chris knows, or suspects, on some level, that his father is suppressing the truth but has an agenda of his own which makes him deny it to others and himself and which makes him break his mother's last grasp on hope.

This, then, is in part a play about repression, about the compromises effected by individuals negotiating between their private needs and their public obligations. Joe is not the only character to substitute the story of his life for his life. They all construct fictions that enable them to justify themselves in their own eyes, as much as in the eyes of others. That is equally true of the neighbors and, beyond them, of a society that generates its own myths about innocence. What we witness is in part a collision of fictions, which are mutually destructive, and, hence, their slow erosion, as what has been repressed begins to force its way to the surface. George Deever is the embodiment of this. He is, Miller insists, the return of the repressed, though the playwright has also acknowledged that "you can't live without denial," that "the truth and mankind are cousins, not brothers and sisters. . . . You have to deny something in order to survive. I think they are all denying something." The difference is that what Joe is denying is a crime. But if George is a reminder of what is being denied he also represents the innocence of the prewar world, when he was a friend and neighbor to the Kellers. He is, Miller has said, "the broken promise of the past."[19]

Such themes, however, are secondary to the principal thrust of the play, whose title is a reflection, as Miller saw it, of John Donne's concept of human solidarity. As he explained in 1999, "The concept behind it was that Joe Keller was both responsible for and a part of a great web of meaning, of being. He had torn that web; he had ripped apart the structure that supports life and society . . . that web of meaning, of existence. And a person who violates it in the way he did has done more than kill a few men. He has killed the possibility of a society having any future, any life. He has destroyed the life-force in that society."[20]

As its title implies, All My Sons is concerned with connective-

ness. What is at stake is the connection between act and conse-
quence, past and present, individual and society, the very concerns, incidentally, to be found in the work of Henrik Ibsen. *The
Pillars of Society*, *Ghosts*, and *The Wild Duck* all turn on concealed
guilt, past crimes, and sudden revelations, which, as in *All My
Sons*, could be said to imply a moral order disturbed and exposed.
But for all Miller's supposedly careful carpentry, there are issues
which he consciously chooses to leave unresolved.

These are people whose flaws, like those in the cylinder heads
supplied by Joe Keller, may have been covered up but still exist. But
Keller's acceptance of culpability is not the only issue in the play.
Meaning is not wholly disclosed, nor is character as neatly aligned
with dramatic function as at times it is in the work of Ibsen. *The Wild
Duck*, for all its virtues, is rather too content to present characters
who are, essentially, defined on their first appearance. There is little,
for example, to be said for Ibsen's sanctimonious Gregers Werle,
who presents his "demand of the ideal," beyond his sanctimony.
Chris Keller's commitment to idealism, by contrast, is carefully motivated, rooted in wartime experience but also tainted with a self-
concern that he is unwilling, and perhaps unable, to address. Gregers
remains unconcerned by the death he provokes; Chris Keller is broken and left with a residue of guilt that cannot easily be discharged.

By the same token, Joe Keller is more deeply mired in denial,
more confused by a world he had taken to be so clear in its neces-
sities, than his counterpart in Ibsen's play. The doctor neighbor,
Relling, in *The Wild Duck*, is there as a humane counterpoint,
cynical but clearheaded; the doctor neighbor in Miller's play is
given a history of his own, an ambivalent marriage and an unresolved tension that make him something more than a marker. And
so it continues: Kate, Ann, and George are not so many pieces in
a jigsaw puzzle, fragments of a completed picture. They are individuals whose motives are deeply ambiguous and whose actions
are suspect even to themselves. We never get to the bottom of this
because they never get to the bottom of it themselves.

This is not a well-made play whose energy is fully discharged with the final pistol shot, whose meaning is wholly revealed in the telling. When, in the final speech, Kate instructs the son, who has just precipitated his own father's death, that he should not "take it on" himself, she is offering him advice wholly at odds with what we have seen in the play—in which the necessity to "take it on" oneself is precisely the point. Why else, finally, does Joe Keller kill himself if not because he does, finally, take it on himself? Only moments before, Chris's mother had asked her son: "Are you trying to kill him?" (84); and the dead son, Larry, has said in a letter, "If I had him there now I could kill him" (83). The death occurs. It does not conclude the play. The guilt survives. Joe's pain (like Larry's) is ended: Chris's is about to begin. He will have to take it on himself. Both are culpable. When Joe cries out, "A man can't be a Jesus in this world!" (83) he hints at a flawed human nature not finally to be resolved by a bullet in the brain. Joe asks of his son that he "see it human." Chris, desperate to recover a lost idealism, fails to do so, and this failure, in its own way, makes him complicit in the very crime he would condemn.

All My Sons expresses the familiar faith of the 1930s in the necessity for human solidarity. The play's true strength, however, comes from the ambivalence that seeps into it. A work that could easily have resolved itself into a moral melodrama which, in stripping away self-deceit and lies and separating performance from actuality, assumed that the residue was untrammeled truth, becomes instead a drama in which motives remain problematic and the demand of the ideal is as suspect as a life lived with no transcendent purpose. It is, finally, a play whose triumph comes precisely from Miller's own ability to "see it human," to embody confused values, flawed ambitions, betrayals, denials, and profound disillusionments, in characters who, fifty and more years later, still speak to us not simply because the issues they embody remain relevant but because blood still beats in their veins.

All My Sons was an immediate and considerable success. It ran for three hundred and twenty-eight performances. In one sense it was a success that scared its author, as he found himself embraced by the very system he had spent more than a decade assaulting. His immediate response was to visit an employment agency in search of manual labor, as if he were at risk of losing touch with a certain authenticity, as if his success were a contaminant. He abandoned the job after a few days. There was no going back. It was also a success, however, that would haunt him in another way as for decades afterward critics generalized about what they took to be his commitment to realism, a commitment which, in truth, he abandoned with his next play, *Death of a Salesman*.

For the truth is that, throughout most of his career, Miller has sought to strike through the pasteboard mask, to explore the way in which what we choose to call reality is a blend of memory and desire, given form and shape by a mind in search of order and self-justification. It is not that he believes we live in a world defined only by competing fictions, though Willy Loman, in *Death of a Salesman*, places his faith in a dream and the stern Puritan judges in *The Crucible* declare their faith in the reality of witches. Rather, reality is clouded by our fears and anxieties, and is constantly re-shaped to serve our psychic and social needs. The details of a crime are indeed laid out for our inspection in *All My Sons*, but this in itself is not the reality of these characters' lives, nor is this a play adequately understood as a realist text. There are many more stories in it than that of a baffled man who, out of a curious admixture of fear and love, single-mindedness and cowardice, commits an act whose implications he refuses to confront.

NOTES

1. Interview with the author for BBC TV, "Miller Shorts" (1999).

2. Arthur Miller, *The Theatre Essays of Arthur Miller*, ed. Robert A. Martin and Steven R. Centola (New York, 1996), p. 133.

3. Arthur Miller, *A View from the Bridge*, *All My Sons* (Harmondsworth, 1961), p. 104.

4. Ibid., p. 129.

5. Ibid., p. 128.

6. Arthur Miller, *Timebends* (London, 1987), p. 134.

7. *Theatre Essays*, p. 128.

8. Ibid., p. 130.

9. Edvard Beyer, *Ibsen: The Man and His Work*, trans. Marie Wells (London, 1978), p. 138.

10. Interview with the author.

11. Arthur Miller, *Collected Plays* (London, 1958), pp. 22, 134.

12. Interview with the author.

13. Clifford Odets, *Golden Boy, Awake and Sing, The Big Knife* (Harmondsworth, 1963), p. 136.

14. Interview with the author.

15. Christopher Bigsby, ed., *Arthur Miller and Company* (London, 1990), p. 50.

16. Interview with the author.

17. Ibid.

18. Ibid.

19. Ibid.

20. Ibid.

ALL MY SONS

FOR ELIA KAZAN

All My Sons was first presented by Elia Kazan, Harold Clurman, and Walter Fried (in association with Herbert Harris), at the Coronet Theatre on the evening of January 29, 1947, with the following cast:

JOE KELLER	Ed Begley
KATE KELLER	Beth Merrill
CHRIS KELLER	Arthur Kennedy
ANN DEEVER	Lois Wheeler
GEORGE DEEVER	Karl Malden
DR. JIM BAYLISS	John McGovern
SUE BAYLISS	Peggy Meredith
FRANK LUBEY	Dudley Sadler
LYDIA LUBEY	Hope Cameron
BERT	Eugene Steiner

The production was directed by Elia Kazan.
The setting was designed by Mordecai Gorelik.

SYNOPSIS OF SCENES

ACT I
The back yard of the Keller home in the out-skirts of an American town. August of our era.

ACT II
Scene, as before. The same evening,
as twilight falls.

ACT III
Scene, as before.
Two o'clock the following morning.

ACT ONE

The back yard of the KELLER *home in the outskirts of an American town. August of our era.*

The stage is hedged on R. *and* L. *by tall, closely planted poplars which lend the yard a secluded atmosphere. Upstage is filled with the back of the house and its open, unroofed porch which extends into the yard some six feet. The house is two stories high and has seven rooms. It would have cost perhaps fifteen thousand in the early twenties when it was built. Now it is nicely painted, looks tight and comfortable, and the yard is green with sod, here and there plants whose season is gone. At the* R., *beside the house, the entrance of the driveway can be seen, but the poplars cut off view of its continuation downstage. In the* L. *corner, downstage, stands the four-foot-high stump of a slender apple tree whose upper trunk and branches lie toppled beside it, fruit still clinging to its branches. Downstage* R. *is a small, trellised arbor, shaped like a sea-shell, with a decorative bulb hanging from its forward-curving roof. Garden chairs and a table are scattered about. A garbage pail on the ground next to the porch steps, a wire leaf-burner near it.*

ON THE RISE: *It is early Sunday morning.* JOE KELLER *is sitting in the sun reading the want ads of the Sunday paper, the other sections of which lie neatly on the ground beside him. Behind his back, inside the arbor,* DOCTOR JIM BAYLISS *is reading part of the paper at the table.*

KELLER *is nearing sixty. A heavy man of stolid mind and build, a business man these many years, but with the imprint of the machine-shop worker and boss still upon him. When he reads,*

*when he speaks, when he listens, it is with the terrible concentration
of the uneducated man for whom there is still wonder in many commonly known things, a man whose judgments must be dredged out
of experience and a peasant-like common sense. A man among men.*

DOCTOR BAYLISS *is nearing forty. A wry self-controlled man,
an easy talker, but with a wisp of sadness that clings even to his
self-effacing humor.*

AT CURTAIN, JIM *is standing at* L., *staring at the broken tree.
He taps a pipe on it, blows through the pipe, feels in his pockets for
tobacco, then speaks.*

JIM: Where's your tobacco?

KELLER: I think I left it on the table. [JIM *goes slowly to table on
the arbor at* R., *finds a pouch, and sits there on the bench, filling his pipe.*]
Gonna rain tonight.

JIM: Paper says so?

KELLER: Yeah, right here.

JIM: Then it can't rain.

[FRANK LUBEY *enters, from* R., *through a small space between the
poplars.* FRANK *is thirty-two but balding. A pleasant, opinionated
man, uncertain of himself, with a tendency toward peevishness
when crossed, but always wanting it pleasant and neighborly. He
rather saunters in, leisurely, nothing to do. He does not notice* JIM
in the arbor. On his greeting, JIM *does not bother looking up.*]

FRANK: Hya.

KELLER: Hello, Frank. What's doin'?

FRANK: Nothin'. Walking off my breakfast. [*Looks up at the sky*]
That beautiful? Not a cloud.

KELLER [*looks up*]: Yeah, nice.

FRANK: Every Sunday ought to be like this.

KELLER [*indicating the sections beside him*]: Want the paper?

FRANK: What's the difference, it's all bad news. What's today's
calamity?

KELLER: I don't know, I don't read the news part any more. It's
more interesting in the want ads.

FRANK: Why, you trying to buy something?

KELLER: No, I'm just interested. To see what people want, y'know? For instance, here's a guy is lookin' for two Newfoundland dogs. Now what's he want with two Newfoundland dogs?

FRANK: That is funny.

KELLER: Here's another one. Wanted—Old Dictionaries. High prices paid. Now what's a man going to do with an old dictionary?

FRANK: Why not? Probably a book collector.

KELLER: You mean he'll make a living out of that?

FRANK: Sure, there's a lot of them.

KELLER [*shakes his head*]: All the kind of business goin' on. In my day, either you were a lawyer, or a doctor, or you worked in a shop. Now . . .

FRANK: Well, I was going to be a forester once.

KELLER: Well, that shows you; in my day, there was no such thing. [*Scanning the page, sweeping it with his hand*] You look at a page like this you realize how ignorant you are. [*Softly, with wonder, as he scans page*] Psss!

FRANK [*noticing tree*]: Hey, what happened to your tree?

KELLER: Ain't that awful? The wind must've got it last night. You heard the wind, didn't you?

FRANK: Yeah, I got a mess in my yard, too. [*Goes to tree*] What a pity. [*Turns to* KELLER] What'd Kate say?

KELLER: They're all asleep yet. I'm just waiting for her to see it.

FRANK [*struck*]: You know?—It's funny.

KELLER: What?

FRANK: Larry was born in August. He'd been twenty-seven this month. And his tree blows down.

KELLER [*touched*]: I'm surprised you remember his birthday, Frank. That's nice.

FRANK: Well, I'm working on his horoscope.

KELLER: How can you make him a horoscope? That's for the future, ain't it?

FRANK: Well, what I'm doing is this, see. Larry was reported missing on November 25th, right?

KELLER: Yeah?

FRANK: Well, then, we assume that if he was killed it was on November 25th. Now, what Kate wants . . .

KELLER: Oh, Kate asked you to make a horoscope?

FRANK: Yeah, what she wants to find out is whether November 25th was a favorable day for Larry.

KELLER: What is that, favorable day?

FRANK: Well, a favorable day for a person is a fortunate day, according to his stars. In other words it would be practically impossible for him to have died on his favorable day.

KELLER: Well, was that his favorable day?—November 25th?

FRANK: That's what I'm working on to find out. It takes time! See, the point is, if November 25th was his favorable day, then it's completely possible he's alive somewhere, because . . . I mean it's possible. [*He notices* JIM *now.* JIM *is looking at him as though at an idiot.* To JIM—*with an uncertain laugh*] I didn't even see you.

KELLER [*to* JIM]: Is he talkin' sense?

JIM: Him? He's all right. He's just completely out of his mind, that's all.

FRANK [*peeved*]: The trouble with you is, you don't *believe* in anything.

JIM: And your trouble is that you believe in *anything. You* didn't see my kid this morning, did you?

FRANK: No.

KELLER: Imagine? He walked off with his thermometer. Right out of his bag.

JIM [*Gets up*]: What a problem. One look at a girl and he takes her temperature. [*Goes to driveway, looks upstage toward street*]

FRANK: That boy's going to be a real doctor; he's smart.

JIM: Over my dead body he'll be a doctor. A good beginning, too.

FRANK. Why? It's an honorable profession.

JIM [*looks at him tiredly*]: Frank, will you stop talking like a civics book? [KELLER *laughs.*]

FRANK: Why, I saw a movie a couple of weeks ago, reminded me of you. There was a doctor in that picture . . .

KELLER: Don Ameche!

FRANK: I think it was, yeah. And he worked in his basement discovering things. That's what you ought to do; you could help humanity, instead of . . .

JIM: I would love to help humanity on a Warner Brothers salary.

KELLER [*points at him, laughing*]: That's very good, Jim.

JIM [*looks toward house*]: Well, where's the beautiful girl was supposed to be here?

FRANK [*excited*]: Annie came?

KELLER: Sure, sleepin' upstairs. We picked her up on the one o'clock train last night. Wonderful thing. Girl leaves here, a scrawny kid. Couple of years go by, she's a regular woman. Hardly recognized her, and she was running in and out of this yard all her life. That was a very happy family used to live in your house, Jim.

JIM: Like to meet her. The block can use a pretty girl. In the whole neighborhood there's not a damned thing to look at. [*Enter* SUE, JIM'S *wife, from* L. *She is rounding forty, an overweight woman who fears it. On seeing her* JIM *wryly adds*] . . . Except my wife, of course.

SUE [*in same spirit*]: Mrs. Adams is on the phone, you dog.

JIM [*to* KELLER]: Such is the condition which prevails [*going to his wife*], my love, my light. . . .

SUE: Don't sniff around me. [*Points to their house,* L.] And give her a nasty answer. I can smell her perfume over the phone.

JIM: What's the matter with her now?

SUE: I don't know, dear. She sounds like she's in terrible pain—unless her mouth is full of candy.

JIM: Why don't you just tell her to lay down?

SUE: She enjoys it more when you tell her to lay down. And when are you going to see Mr. Hubbard?

JIM: My dear; Mr. Hubbard is not sick, and I have better things to do than to sit there and hold his hand.

SUE: It seems to me that for ten dollars you could hold his hand.

JIM [*to* KELLER]: If your son wants to play golf tell him I'm ready. [*Going* L.] Or if he'd like to take a trip around the world for about thirty years. [*He exits* L.]

KELLER: Why do you needle him? He's a doctor, women are supposed to call him up.

SUE: All I said was Mrs. Adams is on the phone. Can I have some of your parsley?

KELLER: Yeah, sure. [*She goes* L. *to parsley box and pulls some parsley*] You were a nurse too long, Susie. You're too . . . too . . . realistic.

SUE [*laughing, points at him*]: Now you said it! [*Enter* LYDIA LUBEY *from* R. *She is a robust, laughing girl of twenty-seven.*]

LYDIA: Frank, the toaster . . . [*Sees the others*] Hya.

KELLER: Hello!

LYDIA [*to* FRANK]: The toaster is off again.

FRANK: Well, plug it in, I just fixed it.

LYDIA [*kindly, but insistently*]: Please, dear, fix it back like it was before.

FRANK: I don't know why you can't learn to turn on a simple thing like a toaster! [FRANK *exits* R.]

SUE [*laughs*]: Thomas Edison.

LYDIA [*apologetically*]: He's really very handy. [*She sees broken tree*] Oh, did the wind get your tree?

KELLER: Yeah, last night.

LYDIA: Oh, what a pity. Annie get in?

KELLER: She'll be down soon. Wait'll you meet her, Sue, she's a knockout.

SUE: I should've been a man. People are always introducing me to beautiful women. [*To* JOE] Tell her to come over later; I imagine she'd like to see what we did with her house. And thanks. [SUE *exits* L.]

LYDIA: Is she still unhappy, Joe?

KELLER: Annie? I don't suppose she goes around dancing on her toes, but she seems to be over it.

LYDIA: She going to get married? Is there anybody . . . ?

KELLER: I suppose . . . say, it's a couple years already. She can't mourn a boy forever.

LYDIA: It's so strange . . . Annie's here and not even married. And I've got three babies. I always thought it'd be the other way around.

KELLER: Well, that's what a war does. I had two sons, now I got one. It changed all the tallies. In my day when you had sons it was an honor. Today a doctor could make a million dollars if he could figure out a way to bring a boy into the world without a trigger finger.

LYDIA: You know, I was just reading . . . [*Enter* CHRIS KELLER *from house, stands in doorway.*]

LYDIA: Hya, Chris . . . [FRANK *shouts from off* R.]

FRANK: Lydia, come in here! If you want the toaster to work don't plug in the malted mixer.

LYDIA [*embarrassed, laughs*]: Did I . . . ?

FRANK: And the next time I fix something don't tell me I'm crazy! Now come in here!

LYDIA [*to* KELLER]: I'll never hear the end of this one.

KELLER [*calling to* FRANK]: So what's the difference? Instead of toast have a malted!

LYDIA: Sh! sh! [*She exits* R. *laughing.*]

[CHRIS *watches her off. He is thirty-two; like his father, solidly built, a listener. A man capable of immense affection and loyalty. He has a cup of coffee in one hand, part of a doughnut in other.*]

KELLER: You want the paper?

CHRIS: That's all right, just the book section. [*He bends down and pulls out part of paper on porch floor.*]

KELLER: You're always reading the book section and you never buy a book.

CHRIS [*coming down to settee*]: I like to keep abreast of my ignorance. [*He sits on settee.*]

KELLER: What is that, every week a new book comes out?

CHRIS: Lot of new books.

KELLER: All different.

CHRIS: All different.

KELLER [*shakes his head, puts knife down on bench, takes oilstone up to the cabinet*]: Psss! Annie up yet?

CHRIS: Mother's giving her breakfast in the dining-room.

KELLER [*crosses, D.S. of stool, looking at broken tree*]: See what happened to the tree?

CHRIS [*without looking up*]: Yeah.

KELLER: What's Mother going to say? [BERT *runs on from driveway. He is about eight. He jumps on stool, then on* KELLER'S *back.*]

BERT: You're finally up.

KELLER [*swinging him around and putting him down*]: Ha! Bert's here! Where's Tommy? He's got his father's thermometer again.

BERT: He's taking a reading.

CHRIS: What!

BERT: But it's only oral.

KELLER: Oh, well, there's no harm in oral. So what's new this morning, Bert?

BERT: Nothin'. [*He goes to broken tree, walks around it.*]

KELLER: Then you couldn't've made a complete inspection of the block. In the beginning, when I first made you a policeman you used to come in every morning with something new. Now, nothin's ever new.

BERT: Except some kids from Thirtieth Street. They started kicking a can down the block, and I made them go away because you were sleeping.

KELLER: Now you're talkin', Bert. Now you're on the ball. First thing you know I'm liable to make you a detective.

BERT [*pulls him down by the lapel and whispers in his ear*]: Can I see the jail now?

KELLER: Seein' the jail ain't allowed, Bert. You know that.

BERT: Aw, I betcha there isn't even a jail. I don't see any bars on the cellar windows.

KELLER: Bert, on my word of honor, there's a jail in the basement. I showed you my gun, didn't I?

BERT: But that's a hunting gun.

KELLER: That's an arresting gun!

BERT: Then why don't you ever arrest anybody? Tommy said another dirty word to Doris yesterday, and you didn't even demote him.

KELLER [*he chuckles and winks at* CHRIS, *who is enjoying all this*]: Yeah, that's a dangerous character, that Tommy. [*Beckons him closer*] What word does he say?

BERT [*backing away quickly in great embarrassment*]: Oh, I can't say that.

KELLER [*grabs him by the shirt and pulls him back*]: Well, gimme an idea.

BERT: I can't. It's not a nice word.

KELLER: Just whisper it in my ear. I'll close my eyes. Maybe I won't even hear it.

BERT [*on tiptoe, puts his lips to* KELLER'S *ear, then in unbearable embarrassment steps back*]: I can't, Mr. Keller.

CHRIS [*laughing*]: Don't make him do that.

KELLER: Okay, Bert. I take your word. Now go out, and keep both eyes peeled.

BERT [*interested*]: For what?

KELLER: For what! Bert, the whole neighborhood is depending on you. A policeman don't ask questions. Now peel them eyes!

BERT [*mystified, but willing*]: Okay. [*He runs off* R. *back of arbor.*]

KELLER [*calling after him*]: And mum's the word, Bert.

BERT [*stops and sticks his head thru the arbor*]: About what?

KELLER: Just in general. Be v-e-r-y careful.

BERT [*nods in bewilderment*]: Okay. [BERT *exits* D.R.]

KELLER [*laughs*]: I got all the kids crazy!

CHRIS: One of these days, they'll all come in here and beat your brains out.

KELLER: What's she going to say? Maybe we ought to tell her before she sees it.

CHRIS: She saw it.

KELLER: How could she see it? I was the first one up. She was still in bed.

CHRIS: She was out here when it broke.

KELLER: When?

CHRIS: About four this morning. [*Indicating window above them*] I heard it cracking and I woke up and looked out. She was standing right here when it cracked.

KELLER: What was she doing out here four in the morning?

CHRIS: I don't know. When it cracked she ran back into the house and cried in the kitchen.

KELLER: Did you talk to her?

CHRIS: No, I . . . I figured the best thing was to leave her alone. [*Pause.*]

KELLER [*deeply touched*]: She cried hard?

CHRIS: I could hear her right through the floor of my room.

KELLER [*slight pause*]: What was she doing out here at that hour? [CHRIS *silent. An undertone of anger showing.*] She's dreaming about him again. She's walking around at night.

CHRIS: I guess she is.

KELLER: She's getting just like after he died. [*Slight pause*] What's the meaning of that?

CHRIS: I don't know the meaning of it. [*Slight pause*] But I know one thing, Dad. We've made a terrible mistake with Mother.

KELLER: What?

CHRIS: Being dishonest with her. That kind of thing always pays off, and now it's paying off.

KELLER: What do you mean, dishonest?

CHRIS: You know Larry's not coming back and I know it. Why do we allow her to go on thinking that we believe with her?

KELLER: What do you want to do, argue with her?

CHRIS: I don't want to argue with her, but it's time she realized that nobody believes Larry is alive any more. [KELLER *simply moves away, thinking, looking at the ground.*] Why shouldn't she dream of him, walk the nights waiting for him? Do we contradict her? Do we say straight out that we have no hope any more? That we haven't had any hope for years now?

KELLER [*frightened at the thought*]: You can't say that to her.

CHRIS: We've got to say it to her.

KELLER: How're you going to prove it? Can you prove it?

CHRIS: For God's sake, three years! Nobody comes back after three years. It's insane.

KELLER: To you it is, and to me. But not to her. You can talk yourself blue in the face, but there's no body and there's no grave, so where are you?

CHRIS: Sit down, Dad. I want to talk to you.

KELLER [*looks at him searchingly a moment, and sitting . . .*]: The trouble is the Goddam newspapers. Every month some boy turns up from nowhere, so the next one is going to be Larry, so . . .

CHRIS: All right, all right, listen to me. [*Slight pause. KELLER sits on settee.*] You know why I asked Annie here, don't you?

KELLER [*he knows, but . . .*]: Why?

CHRIS: You know.

KELLER: Well, I got an idea, but . . . What's the story?

CHRIS: I'm going to ask her to marry me. [*Slight pause.*]

KELLER [*nods*]: Well, that's only your business, Chris.

CHRIS: You know it's not only my business.

KELLER: What do you want me to do? You're old enough to know your own mind.

CHRIS [*asking, annoyed*]: Then it's all right, I'll go ahead with it?

KELLER: Well, you want to be sure Mother isn't going to . . .

CHRIS: Then it isn't just my business.

KELLER: I'm just sayin'. . . .

CHRIS: Sometimes you infuriate me, you know that? Isn't it

your business, too, if I tell this to Mother and she throws a fit about it? You have such a talent for ignoring things.

KELLER: I ignore what I gotta ignore. The girl is Larry's girl . . .

CHRIS: She's not Larry's girl.

KELLER: From Mother's point of view he is not dead and you have no right to take his girl. [*Slight pause*] Now you can go on from there if you know where to go, but I'm tellin' you I don't know where to go. See? I don't know. Now what can I do for you?

CHRIS: I don't know why it is, but every time I reach out for something I want, I have to pull back because other people will suffer. My whole bloody life, time after time after time.

KELLER: You're a considerate fella, there's nothing wrong in that.

CHRIS: To hell with that.

KELLER: Did you ask Annie yet?

CHRIS: I wanted to get this settled first.

KELLER: How do you know she'll marry you? Maybe she feels the same way Mother does?

CHRIS: Well, if she does, then that's the end of it. From her letters I think she's forgotten him. I'll find out. And then we'll thrash it out with Mother? Right? Dad, don't avoid me.

KELLER: The trouble is, you don't see enough women. You never did.

CHRIS: So what? I'm not fast with women.

KELLER: I don't see why it has to be Annie. . . .

CHRIS: Because it is.

KELLER. That's a good answer, but it don't answer anything. You haven't seen her since you went to war. It's five years.

CHRIS. I can't help it. I know her best. I was brought up next door to her. These years when I think of someone for my wife, I think of Annie. What do you want, a diagram?

KELLER. I don't want a diagram . . . I . . . I'm . . . She thinks he's coming back, Chris. You marry that girl and you're pronouncing him dead. Now what's going to happen to Mother? Do you know? I don't! [*Pause.*]

CHRIS: All right, then, Dad.

KELLER [*thinking Chris has retreated*]: Give it some more thought.

CHRIS: I've given it three years of thought. I'd hoped that if I waited, Mother would forget Larry and then we'd have a regular wedding and everything happy. But if that can't happen here, then I'll have to get out.

KELLER: What the hell is *this*?

CHRIS: I'll get out. I'll get married and live someplace else. Maybe in New York.

KELLER: Are you crazy?

CHRIS: I've been a good son too long, a good sucker. I'm through with it.

KELLER: You've got a business here, what the hell is this?

CHRIS: The business! The business doesn't inspire me.

KELLER: Must you be inspired?

CHRIS: Yes. I like it an hour a day. If I have to grub for money all day long at least at evening I want it beautiful. I want a family, I want some kids, I want to build something I can give myself to. Annie is in the middle of that. Now . . . where do I find it?

KELLER: You mean . . . [*Goes to him*] Tell me something, you mean you'd leave the business?

CHRIS: Yes. On this I would.

KELLER [*pause*]: Well . . . you don't want to think like that.

CHRIS: Then help me stay here.

KELLER: All right, but . . . but don't think like that. Because what the hell did I work for? That's only for you, Chris, the whole shootin'-match is for you!

CHRIS: I know that, Dad. Just you help me stay here.

KELLER [*puts a fist up to* CHRIS'S *jaw*]: But don't think that way, you hear me?

CHRIS: I am thinking that way.

KELLER [*lowering his hand*]: I don't understand you, do I?

CHRIS: No, you don't. I'm a pretty tough guy.

KELLER: Yeah. I can see that. [MOTHER *appears on porch. She is in her early fifties, a woman of uncontrolled inspirations, and an overwhelming capacity for love.*]

MOTHER: Joe?

CHRIS [*going toward porch*]: Hello, Mom.

MOTHER [*indicating house behind her. To* KELLER]: Did you take a bag from under the sink?

KELLER: Yeah, I put it in the pail.

MOTHER: Well, get it out of the pail. That's my potatoes. [CHRIS *bursts out laughing—goes up into alley.*]

KELLER [*laughing*]: I thought it was garbage.

MOTHER: Will you do me a favor, Joe? Don't be helpful.

KELLER: I can afford another bag of potatoes.

MOTHER: Minnie scoured that pail in boiling water last night. It's cleaner than your teeth.

KELLER: And I don't understand why, after I worked forty years and I got a maid, why I have to take out the garbage.

MOTHER: If you would make up your mind that every bag in the kitchen isn't full of garbage you wouldn't be throwing out my vegetables. Last time it was the onions. [CHRIS *comes on, hands her bag.*]

KELLER: I don't like garbage in the house.

MOTHER: Then don't eat. [*She goes into the kitchen with bag.*]

CHRIS: That settles you for today.

KELLER: Yeah, I'm in last place again. I don't know, once upon a time I used to think that when I got money again I would have a maid and my wife would take it easy. Now I got money, and I got a maid, and my wife is workin' for the maid. [*He sits in one of the chairs.* MOTHER *comes out on last line. She carries a pot of string-beans.*]

MOTHER: It's her day off, what are you crabbing about?

CHRIS [*to* MOTHER]: Isn't Annie finished eating?

MOTHER [*looking around preoccupiedly at yard*]: She'll be right out. [*Moves*] That wind did some job on this place. [*Of the tree*] So much for that, thank God.

KELLER [*indicating chair beside him*]: Sit down, take it easy.

MOTHER [*she presses her hand to top of her head*]: I've got such a funny pain on the top of my head.

CHRIS: Can I get you an aspirin?

MOTHER [*picks a few petals off ground, stands there smelling them in her hand, then sprinkles them over plants*]: No more roses. It's so funny . . . everything decides to happen at the same time. This month is his birthday; his tree blows down, Annie comes. Everything that happened seems to be coming back. I was just down the cellar, and what do I stumble over? His baseball glove. I haven't seen it in a century.

CHRIS: Don't you think Annie looks well?

MOTHER: Fine. There's no question about it. She's a beauty . . . I still don't know what brought her here. Not that I'm not glad to see her, but . . .

CHRIS: I just thought we'd all like to see each other again. [MOTHER *just looks at him, nodding ever so slightly—almost as though admitting something.*] And I wanted to see her myself.

MOTHER [*her nods halt. To* KELLER]: The only thing is I think her nose got longer. But I'll always love that girl. She's one that didn't jump into bed with somebody else as soon as it happened with her fella.

KELLER [*as though that were impossible for Annie*]: Oh, what're you . . . ?

MOTHER: Never mind. Most of them didn't wait till the telegrams were opened. I'm just glad she came, so you can see I'm not *completely* out of my mind. [*Sits, and rapidly breaks stringbeans in the pot.*]

CHRIS: Just because she isn't married doesn't mean she's been mourning Larry.

MOTHER [*with an undercurrent of observation*]: Why then isn't she?

CHRIS [*a little flustered*]: Well . . . it could've been any number of things.

MOTHER [*directly at him*]: Like what, for instance?

CHRIS [*embarrassed, but standing his ground*]: I don't know. Whatever it is. Can I get you an aspirin? [MOTHER *puts her hand to her head.*]

MOTHER [*she gets up and goes aimlessly toward the trees on rising*]: It's not like a headache.

KELLER: You don't sleep, that's why. She's wearing out more bedroom slippers than shoes.

MOTHER: I had a terrible night. [*She stops moving.*] I never had a night like that.

CHRIS [*looks at* KELLER]: What was it, Mom? Did you dream?

MOTHER: More, more than a dream.

CHRIS [*hesitantly*]: About Larry?

MOTHER: I was fast asleep, and . . . [*Raising her arm over the audience*] Remember the way he used to fly low past the house when he was in training? When we used to see his face in the cockpit going by? That's the way I saw him. Only high up. Way, way up, where the clouds are. He was so real I could reach out and touch him. And suddenly he started to fall. And crying, crying to me . . . Mom, Mom! I could hear him like he was in the room. Mom! . . . it was his voice! If I could touch him I knew I could stop him, if I could only . . . [*Breaks off, allowing her outstretched hand to fall*] I woke up and it was so funny . . . The wind . . . it was like the roaring of his engine. I came out here . . . I must've still been half asleep. I could hear that roaring like he was going by. The tree snapped right in front of me . . . and I like . . . came awake. [*She is looking at tree. She suddenly realizes something, turns with a reprimanding finger shaking slightly at* KELLER.] See? We should never have planted that tree. I said so in the first place; It was too soon to plant a tree for him.

CHRIS [*alarmed*]: Too soon!

MOTHER [*angering*]: We rushed into it. Everybody was in such a hurry to bury him. I *said* not to plant it yet. [*To* KELLER] I *told* you to . . . !

CHRIS: Mother, Mother! [*She looks into his face.*] The wind blew it down. What significance has that got? What are you talking about? Mother, please . . . Don't go through it all again, will you? It's no good, it doesn't accomplish anything. I've been thinking, y'know?—maybe we ought to put our minds to forgetting him?

MOTHER: That's the third time you've said that this week.

CHRIS: Because it's not right; we never took up our lives again. We're like at a railroad station waiting for a train that never comes in.

MOTHER [*presses top of her head*]: Get me an aspirin, heh?

CHRIS: Sure, and let's break out of this, heh, Mom? I thought the four of us might go out to dinner a couple of nights, maybe go dancing out at the shore.

MOTHER: Fine. [*To* KELLER] We can do it tonight.

KELLER: Swell with me!

CHRIS: Sure, let's have some fun. [*To* MOTHER] You'll start with this aspirin. [*He goes up and into house with new spirit. Her smile vanishes.*]

MOTHER [*with an accusing undertone*]: Why did he invite her here?

KELLER: Why does that bother you?

MOTHER: She's been in New York three and a half years, why all of a sudden . . . ?

KELLER: Well, maybe . . . maybe he just wanted to see her . . .

MOTHER: Nobody comes seven hundred miles "just to see."

KELLER: What do you mean? He lived next door to the girl all his life, why shouldn't he want to see her again? [MOTHER *looks at him critically.*] Don't look at me like that, he didn't tell me any more than he told you.

MOTHER [*a warning and a question*]: He's not going to marry her.

KELLER: How do you know he's even thinking of it?

MOTHER: It's got that about it.

KELLER [*sharply watching her reaction*]: Well? So what?

MOTHER [*alarmed*]: What's going on here, Joe?

KELLER: Now listen, kid . . .

MOTHER [*avoiding contact with him*]: She's not his girl, Joe; she knows she's not.

KELLER: You can't read her mind.

MOTHER: Then why is she still single? New York is full of men, why isn't she married? [*Pause*] Probably a hundred people told her she's foolish, but she's waited.

KELLER: How do you know why she waited?

MOTHER: She knows what I know, that's why. She's faithful as a rock. In my worst moments, I think of her waiting, and I know again that I'm right.

KELLER: Look, it's a nice day. What are we arguing for?

MOTHER [*warningly*]: Nobody in this house dast take her faith away, Joe. Strangers might. But not his father, not his brother.

KELLER [*exasperated*]: What do you want me to do? What do you want?

MOTHER: I want you to act like he's coming back. Both of you. Don't think I haven't noticed you since Chris invited her. I won't stand for any nonsense.

KELLER: But, Kate . . .

MOTHER: Because if he's not coming back, then I'll kill my-self! Laugh. Laugh at me. [*She points to tree*] But why did that happen the very night she came back? Laugh, but there are meanings in such things. She goes to sleep in his room and his memorial breaks in pieces. Look at it; look. [*She sits on bench at his* L.] Joe . . .

KELLER: Calm yourself.

MOTHER: Believe with me, Joe. I can't stand all alone.

KELLER: Calm yourself.

MOTHER: Only last week a man turned up in Detroit, missing longer than Larry. You read it yourself.

KELLER: All right, all right, calm yourself.

MOTHER: You above all have got to believe, you . . .

KELLER [*rises*]: Why me above all?

MOTHER: . . . Just don't stop believing . . .

KELLER: What does that mean, me above all? [BERT *comes rushing on from* L.]

BERT: Mr. Keller! Say, Mr. Keller . . . [*Pointing up driveway*] Tommy just said it again!

KELLER [*not remembering any of it*]: Said what? . . . Who? . . .

BERT: The dirty word.

KELLER: Oh. Well . . .

BERT: Gee, aren't you going to arrest him? I warned him.

MOTHER [*with suddenness*]: Stop that, Bert. Go home. [BERT *backs up, as she advances.*] There's no jail here.

KELLER [*As though to say, "Oh-what-the-hell-let-him-believe-there-is"*]: Kate . . .

MOTHER [*turning on* KELLER, *furiously*]: There's no jail here! I want you to stop that jail business! [*He turns, shamed, but peeved.*]

BERT [*past her to* KELLER]: He's right across the street . . .

MOTHER: Go home, Bert. [BERT *turns around and goes up driveway. She is shaken. Her speech is bitten off, extremely urgent.*] I want you to stop that, Joe. That whole jail business!

KELLER [*alarmed, therefore angered*]: Look at you, look at you shaking.

MOTHER [*trying to control herself, moving about clasping her hands*]: I can't help it.

KELLER: What have I got to hide? What the hell is the matter with you, Kate?

MOTHER: I didn't say you had anything to hide, I'm just telling you to stop it! Now stop it! [*As* ANN *and* CHRIS *appear on porch.* ANN *is twenty-six, gentle but despite herself capable of holding fast to what she knows.* CHRIS *opens door for her.*]

ANN: Hya, Joe! [*She leads off a general laugh that is not self-conscious because they know one another too well.*]

CHRIS [*bringing* ANN *down, with an outstretched, chivalric arm*]:

Take a breath of that air, kid. You never get air like that in New York.

MOTHER [*genuinely overcome with it*]: Annie, where did you get that dress!

ANN: I couldn't resist. I'm taking it right off before I ruin it. [*Swings around*] How's that for three weeks' salary?

MOTHER [*to* KELLER]: Isn't she the most . . . ? [*To* ANN] It's gorgeous, simply gor . . .

CHRIS [*to* MOTHER]: No kidding, now, isn't she the prettiest gal you ever saw?

MOTHER [*caught short by his obvious admiration, she finds herself reaching out for a glass of water and aspirin in his hand, and . . .*]: You gained a little weight, didn't you, darling? [*She gulps pill and drinks.*]

ANN: It comes and goes.

KELLER: Look how nice her legs turned out!

ANN [*She runs to fence,* L.]: Boy, the poplars got thick, didn't they?

KELLER [*moves* U. *to settee and sits*]: Well, it's three years, Annie. We're gettin' old, kid.

MOTHER: How does Mom like New York? [ANN *keeps looking through trees.*]

ANN [*a little hurt*]: Why'd they take our hammock away?

KELLER: Oh, no, it broke. Couple of years ago.

MOTHER: What broke? He had one of his light lunches and flopped into it.

ANN [*she laughs and turns back toward* JIM'S *yard. . . .*]: Oh, excuse me! [JIM *has come to fence and is looking over it. He is smoking a cigar. As she cries out, he comes on around on stage.*]

JIM: How do you do. [*To* CHRIS] She looks very intelligent!

CHRIS: Ann, this is Jim . . . Doctor Bayliss.

ANN [*shaking* JIM'S *hand*]: Oh sure, he writes a lot about you.

JIM: Don't believe it. He likes everybody. In the Battalion he was known as Mother McKeller.

ANN: I can believe it . . . You know———? [*To* MOTHER] It's so strange seeing him come out of that yard. [*To* CHRIS] I guess I never grew up. It almost seems that Mom and Pop are in there now. And you and my brother doing Algebra, and Larry trying to copy my home-work. Gosh, those dear dead days beyond recall.

JIM: Well, I hope that doesn't mean you want me to move out?

SUE [*calling from off* L.]: Jim, come in here! Mr. Hubbard is on the phone!

JIM: I told you I don't want . . .

SUE [*commandingly sweet*]: Please, dear! Please!!

JIM [*resigned*]: All right, Susie, [*Trailing off*] all right, all right. . . . [*To* ANN] I've only met you, Ann, but if I may offer you a piece of advice—When you marry, never—even in your mind—never count your husband's money.

SUE [*from off*]: Jim?!

JIM: At once! [*Turns and goes* L.] At once. [*He exits* L.]

MOTHER [ANN *is looking at her. She speaks meaningfully*]: I told her to take up the guitar. It'd be a common interest for them. [*They laugh.*] Well, he loves the guitar!

ANN [*as though to overcome* MOTHER, *she becomes suddenly lively, crosses to* KELLER *on settee, sits on his lap*]: Let's eat at the shore tonight! Raise some hell around here, like we used to before Larry went!

MOTHER [*emotionally*]: You think of him! You see? [*Triumphantly*] She thinks of him!

ANN [*with an uncomprehending smile*]: What do you mean, Kate?

MOTHER: Nothing. Just that you . . . remember him, he's in your thoughts.

ANN: That's a funny thing to say; how could I help remembering him?

MOTHER [*it is drawing to a head the wrong way for her; she starts anew. She rises and comes to* ANN]: Did you hang up your things?

ANN: Yeah . . . [*To* CHRIS] Say, you've sure gone in for clothes. I could hardly find room in the closet.

MOTHER: No, don't you remember? That's Larry's room.

ANN: You mean . . . they're Larry's?

MOTHER: Didn't you recognize them?

ANN [*slowly rising, a little embarrassed*]: Well, it never occurred to me that you'd . . . I mean the shoes are all shined.

MOTHER: Yes, dear. [*Slight pause.* ANN *can't stop staring at her.* MOTHER *breaks it by speaking with the relish of gossip, putting her arm around* ANN *and walking* S.L. *with her.*] For so long I've been aching for a nice conversation with you, Annie. Tell me something.

ANN: What?

MOTHER: I don't know. Something nice.

CHRIS [*wryly*]: She means do you go out much?

MOTHER: Oh, shut up.

KELLER: And are any of them serious?

MOTHER [*laughing, sits in her chair*]: Why don't you both choke?

KELLER: Annie, you can't go into a restaurant with that woman any more. In five minutes thirty-nine strange people are sitting at the table telling her their life story.

MOTHER: If I can't ask Annie a personal question . . .

KELLER: Askin' is all right, but don't beat her over the head. You're beatin' her, you're beatin' her. [*They are laughing.*]

ANN [*to* MOTHER. *Takes pan of beans off stool, puts them on floor under chair and sits*]: Don't let them bulldoze you. Ask me anything you like. What do you want to know, Kate? Come on, let's gossip.

MOTHER [*to* CHRIS *and* KELLER]: She's the only one is got any sense. [*To* ANN] Your mother . . . she's not getting a divorce, heh?

ANN: No, she's calmed down about it now. I think when he gets out they'll probably live together. In New York, of course.

MOTHER: That's fine. Because your father is still . . . I mean he's a decent man after all is said and done.

ANN: I don't care. She can take him back if she likes.

MOTHER: And you? You . . . [*Shakes her head negatively*] . . . go out much? [*Slight pause.*]

ANN [*delicately*]: You mean am I still waiting for him?

MOTHER: Well, no, I don't expect you to wait for him but . . .

ANN [*kindly*]: But that's what you mean, isn't it?

MOTHER: . . . Well . . . yes.

ANN: Well, I'm not, Kate.

MOTHER [*faintly*]: You're not?

ANN: Isn't it ridiculous? You don't really imagine he's . . . ?

MOTHER: I know, dear, but don't say it's ridiculous, because the papers were full of it; I don't know about New York, but there was half a page about a man missing even longer than Larry, and he turned up from Burma.

CHRIS [*coming to* ANN]: He couldn't have wanted to come home very badly, Mom.

MOTHER: Don't be so smart.

CHRIS: You can have a helluva time in Burma.

ANN [*rises and swings around in back of* CHRIS]: So I've heard.

CHRIS: Mother, I'll bet you money that you're the only woman in the country who after three years is still . . .

MOTHER: You're sure?

CHRIS: Yes, I am.

MOTHER: Well, if you're sure then you're sure. [*She turns her head away an instant*] They don't say it on the radio but I'm sure that in the dark at night they're still waiting for their sons.

CHRIS: Mother, you're absolutely——

MOTHER [*waving him off*]: Don't be so damned smart! Now stop it! [*Slight pause*] There are just a few things you *don't* know. All of you. And I'll tell you one of them, Annie. Deep, deep in your heart you've always been waiting for him.

ANN [*resolutely*]: No, Kate.

MOTHER [*with increasing demand*]: But deep in your heart, Annie!

CHRIS: She ought to know, shouldn't she?

MOTHER: Don't let them tell you what to think. Listen to your heart. Only your heart.

ANN: Why does your heart tell you he's alive?

MOTHER: Because he has to be.

ANN: But why, Kate?

MOTHER [*going to her*]: Because certain things have to be, and certain things can never be. Like the sun has to rise, it has to be. That's why there's God. Otherwise anything could happen. But there's God, so certain things can never happen. I would know, Annie—just like I knew the day he [*indicates* CHRIS] went into that terrible battle. Did he write me? Was it in the papers? No, but that morning I couldn't raise my head off the pillow. Ask Joe. Suddenly, I knew! I knew! And he was nearly killed that day. Ann, you *know* I'm right!

ANN [*she stands there in silence, then turns trembling, going upstage*]: No, Kate.

MOTHER: I have to have some tea. [FRANK *appears from* L. *carrying ladder.*]

FRANK: Annie! [*Coming down*] How are you, gee whiz!

ANN [*taking his hand*]: Why, Frank, you're losing your hair.

KELLER: He's got responsibility.

FRANK: Gee whiz!

KELLER: Without Frank the stars wouldn't know when to come out.

FRANK [*laughs. To* ANN]: You look more womanly. You've matured. You . . .

KELLER: Take it easy, Frank, you're a married man.

ANN [*as they laugh*]: You still haberdashering?

FRANK: Why not? Maybe I too can get to be president. How's your brother? Got his degree, I hear.

ANN: Oh, George has his own office now!

FRANK: Don't say! [*Funereally*] And your dad? Is he . . . ?

ANN [*abruptly*]: Fine. I'll be in to see Lydia.

FRANK [*sympathetically*]: How about it, does Dad expect a parole soon?

ANN [*with growing ill-ease*]: I really don't know, I . . .

FRANK [*staunchly defending her father for her sake*]: I mean because I feel, y'know, that if an intelligent man like your father is put in prison, there ought to be a law that says either you execute him, or let him go after a year.

CHRIS [*interrupting*]: Want a hand with that ladder, Frank?

FRANK [*taking cue*]: That's all right, I'll . . . [*Picks up ladder*] I'll finish the horoscope tonight, Kate. [*Embarrassed*] See you later, Ann, you look wonderful. [*He exits* R. *They look at* ANN.]

ANN [*to* CHRIS, *sits slowly on stool*]: Haven't they stopped talking about Dad?

CHRIS [*comes down and sits on arm of chair*]: Nobody talks about him any more.

KELLER [*rises and comes to her*]: Gone and forgotten, kid.

ANN: Tell me. Because I don't want to meet anybody on the block if they're going to . . .

CHRIS: I don't want you to worry about it.

ANN [*to* KELLER]: Do they still remember the case, Joe? Do they talk about you?

KELLER: The only one still talks about it is my wife.

MOTHER: That's because you keep on playing policeman with the kids. All their parents hear out of you is jail, jail, jail.

KELLER: Actually what happened was that when I got home from the penitentiary the kids got very interested in me. You know kids. I was [*Laughs*] like the expert on the jail situation. And as time passed they got it confused and . . . I ended up a detective. [*Laughs.*]

MOTHER: Except that *they* didn't get it confused. [*To* ANN] He hands out police badges from the Post Toasties boxes. [*They laugh.*]

ANN [*wondrously at them, happily. She rises and comes to* KELLER, *putting her arm around his shoulder*]: Gosh, it's wonderful to hear you laughing about it.

CHRIS: Why, what'd you expect?

ANN: The last thing I remember on this block was one word—

"Murderers!" Remember that, Kate? . . . Mrs. Hammond standing in front of our house and yelling that word . . . She's still around, I suppose?

MOTHER: They're all still around.

KELLER: Don't listen to her. Every Saturday night the whole gang is playin' poker in this arbor. All the ones who yelled murderer takin' my money now.

MOTHER: Don't, Joe, she's a sensitive girl, don't fool her. [*To* ANN] They still remember about Dad. It's different with him—[*Indicates* JOE]—he was exonerated, your father's still there. That's why I wasn't so enthusiastic about your coming. Honestly, I know how sensitive you are, and I told Chris, I said . . .

KELLER: Listen, you do like I did and you'll be all right. The day I come home, I got out of my car;—but not in front of the house . . . on the corner. You should've been here, Annie, and you too, Chris; you'd-a seen something. Everybody knew I was getting out that day; the porches were loaded. Picture it now; none of them believed I was innocent. The story was, I pulled a fast one getting myself exonerated. So I get out of my car, and I walk down the street. But very slow. And with a smile. The beast! I was the beast; the guy who sold cracked cylinder heads to the Army Air Force; the guy who made twenty-one P-40's crash in Australia. Kid, walkin' down the street that day I was guilty as hell. Except I wasn't, and there was a court paper in my pocket to prove I wasn't, and I walked . . . past . . . the porches. Result? Fourteen months later I had one of the best shops in the state again, a respected man again; bigger than ever.

CHRIS [*with admiration*]: Joe McGuts.

KELLER [*now with great force*]: That's the only way you lick 'em is guts! [*To* ANN] The worst thing you did was to move away from here. You made it tough for your father when he gets out. That's why I tell you, I like to see him move back right on this block.

MOTHER [*pained*]: How could they move back?

KELLER: It ain't gonna end *till* they move back! [*To* ANN] Till people play cards with him again, and talk with him, and smile with him—you play cards with a man you know he can't be a murderer. And the next time you write him I like you to tell him just what I said. [ANN *simply stares at him*.] You hear me?

ANN [*surprised*]: Don't you hold anything against him?

KELLER: Annie, I never believed in crucifying people.

ANN [*mystified*]: But he was your partner, he dragged you through the mud . . .

KELLER: Well, he ain't my sweetheart, but you gotta forgive, don't you?

ANN: You, either, Kate? Don't you feel any . . . ?

KELLER [*to* ANN]: The next time you write Dad . . .

ANN: I don't write him.

KELLER [*struck*]: Well every now and then you . . .

ANN [*a little ashamed, but determined*]: No, I've *never* written to him. Neither has my brother. [*To* CHRIS] Say, do you feel this way, too?

CHRIS: He murdered twenty-one pilots.

KELLER: What the hell kinda talk is that?

MOTHER: That's not a thing to say about a man.

ANN: What else can you say? When they took him away I followed him, went to him every visiting day. I was crying all the time. Until the news came about Larry. Then I realized. It's wrong to pity a man like that. Father or no father, there's only one way to look at him. He knowingly shipped out parts that would crash an airplane. And how do you know Larry wasn't one of them?

MOTHER: I was waiting for that. [*Going to her*] As long as you're here, Annie, I want to ask you never to say that again.

ANN: You surprise me. I thought you'd be mad at him.

MOTHER: What your father did had nothing to do with Larry. Nothing.

ANN: But we can't know that.

MOTHER [*striving for control*]: As long as you're here!

ANN [*perplexed*]: But, Kate . . .

MOTHER: Put that out of your head!

KELLER: Because . . .

MOTHER [*quickly to* KELLER]: That's all, that's enough. [*Places her hand on her head*] Come inside now, and have some tea with me. [*She turns and goes up steps.*]

KELLER [*to* ANN]: The one thing you . . .

MOTHER [*sharply*]: He's not dead, so there's no argument! Now come!

KELLER [*angrily*]: In a minute! [MOTHER *turns and goes into house.*] Now look, Annie . . .

CHRIS: All right, Dad, forget it.

KELLER: No, she dasn't feel that way. Annie . . .

CHRIS: I'm sick of the whole subject, now cut it out.

KELLER: You want her to go on like this? [*To* ANN] Those cylinder heads went into P-40's only. What's the matter with you? You know Larry never flew a P-40.

CHRIS: So who flew those P-40's, pigs?

KELLER: The man was a fool, but don't make a murderer out of him. You got no sense? Look what it does to her! [*To* ANN] Listen, you gotta appreciate what was doin' in that shop in the war. The both of you! It was a madhouse. Every half hour the Major callin' for cylinder heads, they were whippin' us with the telephone. The trucks were hauling them away hot, damn near. I mean just try to see it human, see it human. All of a sudden a batch comes out with a crack. That happens, that's the business. A fine, hairline crack. All right, so . . . so he's a little man, your father, always scared of loud voices. What'll the Major say?—Half a day's production shot. . . . What'll I say? You know what I mean? Human. [*He pauses.*] So he takes out his tools and he . . . covers over the cracks. All right . . . that's bad, it's wrong, but that's what a little man does. If I could have gone in that day I'd a told him— junk 'em, Steve, we can afford it. But alone he was afraid. But I know he meant no harm. He believed they'd hold up a hundred percent. That's a mistake, but it ain't murder. You mustn't feel that way about him. You understand me? It ain't right.

ANN [*she regards him a moment*]: Joe, let's forget it.

KELLER: Annie, the day the news came about Larry he was in the next cell to mine . . . Dad. And he cried, Annie . . . he cried half the night.

ANN [*touched*]: He shoulda cried all night. [*Slight pause.*]

KELLER [*almost angered*]: Annie, I do not understand why you . . . !

CHRIS [*breaking in—with nervous urgency*]: Are you going to stop it?!

ANN: Don't yell at him. He just wants everybody happy.

KELLER [*clasps her around waist, smiling*]: That's my sentiments. Can you stand steak?

CHRIS: And champagne!

KELLER: Now you're operatin'! I'll call Swanson's for a table! Big time tonight, Annie!

ANN: Can't scare me.

KELLER [*to CHRIS, pointing at ANN*]: I like that girl. Wrap her up. [*They laugh. Goes up porch.*] You got nice legs, Annie! . . . I want to see everybody drunk tonight. [*Pointing to CHRIS*] Look at him, he's blushin'! [*He exits, laughing, into house.*]

CHRIS [*calling after him*]: Drink your tea, Casanova. [*He turns to ANN.*] Isn't he a great guy?

ANN: You're the only one I know who loves his parents!

CHRIS: I know. It went out of style, didn't it?

ANN [*with a sudden touch of sadness*]: It's all right. It's a good thing. [*She looks about.*] You know? It's lovely here. The air is sweet.

CHRIS [*hopefully*]: You're not sorry you came?

ANN: Not sorry, no. But I'm . . . not going to stay . . .

CHRIS: Why?

ANN: In the first place, your mother as much as told me to go.

CHRIS: Well . . .

ANN: You saw that . . . and then you . . . you've been kind of . . .

CHRIS: What?

ANN: Well . . . kind of embarrassed ever since I got here.

CHRIS: The trouble is I planned on kind of sneaking up on you over a period of a week or so. But they take it for granted that we're all set.

ANN: I knew they would. Your mother anyway.

CHRIS: How did you know?

ANN: From *her* point of view, why else would I come?

CHRIS: Well . . . would you want to? [ANN *studies him.*] I guess you know this is why I asked you to come.

ANN: I guess this is why I came.

CHRIS: Ann, I love you. I love you a great deal. [*Finally*] I love you. [*Pause. She waits.*] I have no imagination . . . that's all I know to tell you. [ANN, *waiting, ready*] I'm embarrassing you. I didn't want to tell it to you here. I wanted some place we'd never been; a place where we'd be brand new to each other. . . . You feel it's wrong here, don't you? This yard, this chair? I want you to be ready for me. I don't want to win you away from anything.

ANN [*putting her arms around him*]: Oh, Chris, I've been ready a long, long time!

CHRIS: Then he's gone forever. You're sure.

ANN: I almost got married two years ago.

CHRIS: . . . why didn't you?

ANN: You started to write to me . . . [*Slight pause.*]

CHRIS: You felt something that far back?

ANN: Every day since!

CHRIS: Ann, why didn't you let me know?

ANN: I was waiting for you, Chris. Till then you never wrote. And when you did, what did you say? You sure can be ambiguous, you know.

CHRIS [*he looks towards house, then at her, trembling*]: Give me a kiss, Ann. Give me a . . . [*They kiss.*] God, I kissed you, Annie, I kissed Annie. How long, how long I've been waiting to kiss you!

ANN: I'll never forgive you. Why did you wait all these years? All I've done is sit and wonder if I was crazy for thinking of you.

CHRIS: Annie, we're going to live now! I'm going to make you so happy. [*He kisses her, but without their bodies touching.*]

ANN [*a little embarrassed*]: Not like that you're not.

CHRIS: I kissed you . . .

ANN: Like Larry's brother. Do it like you, Chris. [*He breaks away from her abruptly.*] What is it, Chris?

CHRIS: Let's drive some place . . . I want to be alone with you.

ANN: No . . . what is it, Chris, your mother?

CHRIS: No . . . nothing like that . . .

ANN: Then what's wrong? . . . Even in your letters, there was something ashamed.

CHRIS: Yes. I suppose I have been. But it's going from me.

ANN: You've got to tell me—

CHRIS: I don't know how to start. [*He takes her hand. He speaks quietly, factually at first.*]

ANN: It wouldn't work this way. [*Slight pause.*]

CHRIS: It's all mixed up with so many other things. . . . You remember, overseas, I was in command of a company?

ANN: Yeah, sure.

CHRIS: Well, I lost them.

ANN: How many?

CHRIS: Just about all.

ANN: Oh, gee!

CHRIS: It takes a little time to toss that off. Because they weren't just men. For instance, one time it'd been raining several days and this kid came to me, and gave me his last pair of dry socks. Put them in my pocket. That's only a little thing . . . but . . . that's the kind of guys I had. They didn't die; they killed themselves for each other. I mean that exactly; a little more selfish and they'd've been here today. And I got an idea—watching them go down. Everything was being destroyed, see, but it seemed to me that one new thing was made. A kind of . . . responsibility. Man for man. You understand me?—To show that, to bring that on to the earth again like some kind of a monument and everyone would feel it standing there, behind him, and it would make a difference to him. [*Pause*] And then I came home and it was incredible. I . . . there was no meaning in it here; the whole thing to them was a kind of a—bus accident. I went to work with Dad, and that rat-race again. I felt . . . what you said . . . ashamed somehow. Because nobody was changed at all. It seemed to make suckers out of a lot of guys. I felt wrong to be alive, to open the bank-book, to drive the new car, to see the new refrigerator. I mean you can take those things out of a war, but when you drive that car you've got to know that it came out of the love a man can have for a man, you've got to be a little better because of that. Otherwise what you have is really loot, and there's blood on it. I didn't want to take any of it. And I guess that included you.

ANN: And you still feel that way?

CHRIS: I want you now, Annie.

ANN: Because you mustn't feel that way any more. Because you have a right to whatever you have. Everything, Chris, understand that? To me, too . . . And the money, there's nothing wrong in your money. Your father put hundreds of planes in the air, you should be proud. A man should be paid for that . . .

CHRIS: Oh Annie, Annie . . . I'm going to make a fortune for you!

KELLER [*offstage*]: Hello . . . Yes. Sure.

ANN [*laughing softly*]: What'll I do with a fortune . . . ? [*They kiss. KELLER enters from house.*]

KELLER [*thumbing toward house*]: Hey, Ann, your brother . . . [*They step apart shyly. KELLER comes down, and wryly . . .*] What is this, Labor Day?

CHRIS [*waving him away, knowing the kidding will be endless*]: All right, all right . . .

ANN: You shouldn't burst out like that.

KELLER: Well, nobody told me it was Labor Day. [*Looks around*] Where's the hot dogs?

CHRIS [*loving it*]: All right. You said it once.

KELLER: Well, as long as I know it's Labor Day from now on, I'll wear a bell around my neck.

ANN [*affectionately*]: He's so subtle!

CHRIS: George Bernard Shaw as an elephant.

KELLER: George!—hey, you kissed it out of my head—your brother's on the phone.

ANN [*surprised*]: My brother?

KELLER: Yeah, George. Long distance.

ANN: What's the matter, is anything wrong?

KELLER: I don't know, Kate's talking to him. Hurry up, she'll cost him five dollars.

ANN [*she takes a step upstage, then comes down toward* CHRIS]: I wonder if we ought to tell your mother yet? I mean I'm not very good in an argument.

CHRIS: We'll wait till tonight. After dinner. Now don't get tense, just leave it to me.

KELLER: What're you telling her?

CHRIS: Go ahead, Ann. [*With misgivings,* ANN *goes up and into house.*] We're getting married, Dad. [KELLER *nods indecisively.*] Well, don't you say anything?

KELLER [*distracted*]: I'm glad, Chris, I'm just . . . George is calling from Columbus.

CHRIS: Columbus!

KELLER: Did Annie tell you he was going to see his father today?

CHRIS: No, I don't think she knew anything about it.

KELLER [*asking uncomfortably*]: Chris! You . . . you think you know her pretty good?

CHRIS [*hurt and apprehensive*]: What kind of a question . . . ?

KELLER: I'm just wondering. All these years George don't go to see his father. Suddenly he goes . . . and she comes here.

CHRIS: Well, what about it?

KELLER: It's crazy, but it comes to my mind. She don't hold nothin' against me, does she?

CHRIS [*angry*]: I don't know what you're talking about.

KELLER [*a little more combatively*]: I'm just talkin'. To his last day in court the man blamed it all on me; and this is his daughter. I mean if she was sent here to find out something?

CHRIS [*angered*]: Why? What is there to find out?

ANN [*on phone, offstage*]: Why are you so excited, George? What happened there?

KELLER: I mean if they want to open up the case again, for the nuisance value, to hurt us?

CHRIS: Dad . . . how could you think that of her? ⎱
ANN [*still on phone*]: But what did he say to you, ⎰ [*Together*]
for God's sake?

KELLER: It couldn't be, heh. You know.

CHRIS: Dad, you amaze me . . .

KELLER [*breaking in*]: All right, forget it, forget it. [*With great force, moving about*] I want a clean start for you, Chris. I want a new sign over the plant—Christopher Keller, Incorporated.

CHRIS [*a little uneasily*]: J. O. Keller is good enough.

KELLER: We'll talk about it. I'm going to build you a house, stone, with a driveway from the road. I want you to spread out, Chris, I want you to use what I made for you . . . [*He is close to him now.*] . . . I mean, with joy, Chris, without shame . . . with joy.

CHRIS [*touched*]: I will, Dad.

KELLER [*with deep emotion*]: . . . Say it to me.

CHRIS: Why?

KELLER: Because sometimes I think you're . . . ashamed of the money.

CHRIS: No, don't feel that.

KELLER: Because it's good money, there's nothing wrong with that money.

CHRIS [*a little frightened*]: Dad, you don't have to tell me this.

KELLER [*with overriding affection and self-confidence now. He grips* CHRIS *by the back of the neck, and with laughter between his determined jaws*]: Look, Chris, I'll go to work on Mother for you. We'll get her so drunk tonight we'll all get married! [*Steps away, with a wide gesture of his arm*] There's gonna be a wedding, kid, like there never was seen! Champagne, tuxedoes . . . !

[*He breaks off as* ANN's *voice comes out loud from the house where she is still talking on phone.*]

ANN: Simply because when you get excited you don't control yourself. . . . [MOTHER *comes out of house.*] Well, what did he tell you for God's sake? [*Pause*] All right, come then. [*Pause*] Yes, they'll all be here. Nobody's running away from you. And try to get hold of yourself, will you? [*Pause*] All right, all right. Goodbye. [*There is a brief pause as Ann hangs up receiver, then comes out of kitchen.*]

CHRIS: Something happen?

KELLER: He's coming here?

ANN: On the seven o'clock. He's in Columbus. [*To* MOTHER] I told him it would be all right.

KELLER: Sure, fine! Your father took sick?

ANN [*mystified*]: No, George didn't say he was sick. I . . . [*Shaking it off*] I don't know, I suppose it's something stupid, you know my brother . . . [*She comes to* CHRIS.] Let's go for a drive, or something . . .

CHRIS: Sure. Give me the keys, Dad.

MOTHER: Drive through the park. It's beautiful now.

CHRIS: Come on, Ann. [*To them*] Be back right away.

ANN [*as she and* CHRIS *exit up driveway*]: See you. [MOTHER *comes down toward Keller, her eyes fixed on him.*]

KELLER: Take your time. [*To* MOTHER] What does George want?

MOTHER: He's been in Columbus since this morning with Steve. He's gotta see Annie right away, he says.

KELLER: What for?

MOTHER: I don't know. [*She speaks with warning.*] He's a lawyer now, Joe. George is a lawyer. All these years he never even sent a postcard to Steve. Since he got back from the war, not a postcard.

KELLER: So what?

MOTHER [*her tension breaking out*]: Suddenly he takes an airplane from New York to see him. An airplane!

KELLER: Well? So?

MOTHER [*trembling*]: Why?

KELLER: I don't read minds. Do you?

MOTHER: Why, Joe? What has Steve suddenly got to tell him that he takes an airplane to see him?

KELLER: What do I care what Steve's got to tell him?

MOTHER: You're sure, Joe?

KELLER [*frightened, but angry*]: Yes, I'm sure.

MOTHER [*she sits stiffly in a chair*]: Be smart now, Joe. The boy is coming. Be smart.

KELLER [*desperately*]: Once and for all, did you hear what I said? I said I'm sure!

MOTHER [*she nods weakly*]: All right, Joe. [*He straightens up.*] Just . . . be smart. [KELLER, *in hopeless fury, looks at her, turns around, goes up to porch and into house, slamming screen door violently behind him.* MOTHER *sits in chair downstage, stiffly, staring, seeing.*]

CURTAIN

ACT TWO

As twilight falls, that evening.

ON THE RISE: CHRIS *is discovered at* R., *sawing the broken-off tree, leaving stump standing alone. He is dressed in good pants, white shoes, but without a shirt. He disappears with tree up the alley when* MOTHER *appears on porch. She comes down and stands watching him. She has on a dressing-gown, carries a tray of grape-juice drink in a pitcher, and glasses with sprigs of mint in them.*

MOTHER [*calling up alley*]: Did you have to put on good pants to do that? [*She comes downstage and puts tray on table in the arbor. Then looks around uneasily, then feels pitcher for coolness.* CHRIS *enters from alley brushing off his hands.*] You notice there's more light with that thing gone?

CHRIS: Why aren't you dressing?

MOTHER: It's suffocating upstairs. I made a grape drink for Georgie. He always liked grape. Come and have some.

CHRIS [*impatiently*]: Well, come on, get dressed. And what's Dad sleeping so much for? [*He goes to table and pours a glass of juice.*]

MOTHER: He's worried. When he's worried he sleeps. [*Pauses. Looks into his eyes*] We're dumb, Chris. Dad and I are stupid people. We don't know anything. You've got to protect us.

CHRIS: You're silly; what's there to be afraid of?

MOTHER: To his last day in court Steve never gave up the idea that Dad made him do it. If they're going to open the case again I won't live through it.

CHRIS: George is just a damn fool, Mother. How can you take him seriously?

MOTHER: That family hates us. Maybe even Annie. . . .

CHRIS: Oh, now, Mother . . .

MOTHER: You think just because you like everybody, they like you!

CHRIS: All right, stop working yourself up. Just leave everything to me.

MOTHER: When George goes home tell her to go with him.

CHRIS [*noncommittally*]: Don't worry about Annie.

MOTHER: Steve is her father, too.

CHRIS: Are you going to cut it out? Now, come.

MOTHER [*going upstage with him*]: You don't realize how people can hate, Chris, they can hate so much they'll tear the world to pieces. . . . [ANN, *dressed up, appears on porch.*]

CHRIS: Look! She's dressed already. [*As he and* MOTHER *mount porch*] I've just got to put on a shirt.

ANN [*in a preoccupied way*]: Are you feeling well, Kate?

MOTHER: What's the difference, dear. There are certain people, y'know, the sicker they get the longer they live. [*She goes into house.*]

CHRIS: You look nice.

ANN: We're going to tell her tonight.

CHRIS: Absolutely, don't worry about it.

ANN: I wish we could tell her now. I can't stand scheming. My stomach gets hard.

CHRIS: It's not scheming, we'll just get her in a better mood.

MOTHER [*offstage, in the house*]: Joe, are you going to sleep all day!

ANN [*laughing*]: The only one who's relaxed is your father. He's fast asleep.

CHRIS: I'm relaxed.

ANN: Are you?

CHRIS: Look. [*He holds out his hand and makes it shake.*] Let me know when George gets here. [*He goes into the house. She moves aimlessly, and then is drawn toward tree stump. She goes to it, hesitantly touches broken top in the hush of her thoughts. Offstage* LYDIA *calls,* "Johnny! Come get your supper!" SUE *enters from* L., *and halts, seeing Ann.*]

SUE: Is my husband . . . ?

ANN [*turns, startled*]: Oh!

SUE: I'm terribly sorry.

ANN: It's all right, I . . . I'm a little silly about the dark.

SUE [*looks about*]: It is getting dark.

ANN: Are you looking for your husband?

SUE: As usual. [*Laughs tiredly*] He spends so much time here, they'll be charging him rent.

ANN: Nobody was dressed so he drove over to the depot to pick up my brother.

SUE: Oh, your brother's in?

ANN: Yeah, they ought to be here any minute now. Will you have a cold drink?

SUE: I will, thanks. [ANN *goes to table and pours.*] My husband. Too hot to drive me to beach.—Men are like little boys; for the neighbors they'll always cut the grass.

ANN: People like to do things for the Kellers. Been that way since I can remember.

SUE: It's amazing. I guess your brother's coming to give you away, heh?

ANN [*giving her drink*]: I don't know. I suppose.

SUE: You must be all nerved up.

ANN: It's always a problem getting yourself married, isn't it?

SUE: That depends on your shape, of course. I don't see why you should have had a problem.

ANN: I've had chances—

SUE: I'll bet. It's romantic . . . it's very unusual to me, marrying the brother of your sweetheart.

ANN: I don't know. I think it's mostly that whenever I need somebody to tell me the truth I've always thought of Chris. When he tells you something you know it's so. He relaxes me.

SUE: And he's got money. That's important, you know.

ANN: It wouldn't matter to me.

SUE: You'd be surprised. It makes all the difference. I married an interne. On my salary. And that was bad, because as soon as a woman supports a man he owes her something. You can never owe somebody without resenting them. [ANN *laughs*.] That's true, you know.

ANN: Underneath, I think the doctor is very devoted.

SUE: Oh, certainly. But it's bad when a man always sees the bars in front of him. Jim thinks he's in jail all the time.

ANN: Oh . . .

SUE: That's why I've been intending to ask you a small favor, Ann . . . it's something very important to me.

ANN: Certainly, if I can do it.

SUE: You can. When you take up housekeeping, try to find a place away from here.

ANN: Are you fooling?

SUE: I'm very serious. My husband is unhappy with Chris around.

ANN: How is that?

SUE: Jim's a successful doctor. But he's got an idea he'd like to do medical research. Discover things. You see?

ANN: Well, isn't that good?

SUE: Research pays twenty-five dollars a week minus laundering the hair shirt. You've got to give up your life to go into it.

ANN: How does Chris?

SUE [*with growing feeling*]: Chris makes people want to be better than it's possible to be. He does that to people.

ANN: Is that bad?

SUE: My husband has a family, dear. Every time he has a session with Chris he feels as though he's compromising by not giving up everything for research. As though Chris or anybody else isn't compromising. It happens with Jim every couple of years. He meets a man and makes a statue out of him.

ANN: Maybe he's right. I don't mean that Chris is a statue, but . . .

SUE: Now darling, you know he's not right.

ANN: I don't agree with you. Chris . . .

SUE: Let's face it, dear. Chris is working with his father, isn't he? He's taking money out of that business every week in the year.

ANN: What of it?

SUE: You ask me what of it?

ANN: I certainly do ask you. [*She seems about to burst out.*] You oughtn't cast aspersions like that, I'm surprised at you.

SUE: You're surprised at me!

ANN: He'd never take five cents out of that plant if there was anything wrong in it.

SUE: You know that.

ANN: I know it. I resent everything you've said.

SUE [*moving toward her*]: You know what I resent, dear?

ANN: Please, I don't want to argue.

SUE: I resent living next door to the Holy Family. It makes me look like a bum, you understand?

ANN: I can't do anything about that.

SUE: Who is he to ruin a man's life? Everybody knows Joe pulled a fast one to get out of jail.

ANN: That's not true!

SUE: Then why don't you go out and talk to people? Go on, talk to them. There's not a person on the block who doesn't know the truth.

ANN: That's a lie. People come here all the time for cards and . . .

SUE: So what? They give him credit for being smart. I do, too, I've got nothing against Joe. But if Chris wants people to put on the hair shirt let him take off his broadcloth. He's driving my husband crazy with that phony idealism of his, and I'm at the end of my rope on it! [CHRIS *enters on porch, wearing shirt and tie now. She turns quickly, hearing. With a smile.*] Hello, darling. How's Mother?

CHRIS: I thought George came.

SUE: No, it was just us.

CHRIS [*coming down to them*]: Susie, do me a favor, heh? Go up to Mother and see if you can calm her. She's all worked up.

SUE: She still doesn't know about you two?

CHRIS [*laughs a little*]: Well, she senses it, I guess. You know my mother.

SUE [*going up to porch*]: Oh, yeah, she's psychic.

CHRIS: Maybe there's something in the medicine chest.

SUE: I'll give her one of everything. [*On porch*] Don't worry about Kate; couple of drinks, dance her around a little . . . she'll love Ann. [*To* ANN] Because you're the female version of him. [CHRIS *laughs.*] Don't be alarmed, I said version. [*She goes into house.*]

CHRIS: Interesting woman, isn't she?

ANN: Yeah, she's very interesting.

CHRIS: She's a great nurse, you know, she . . .

ANN [*in tension, but trying to control it*]: Are you still doing that?

CHRIS [*sensing something wrong, but still smiling*]: Doing what?

ANN: As soon as you get to know somebody you find a distinction for them. How do you know she's a great nurse?

CHRIS: What's the matter, Ann?

ANN: The woman hates you. She despises you!

CHRIS: Hey . . . what's hit you?

ANN: Gee, Chris . . .

CHRIS: What happened here?

ANN: You never . . . Why didn't you tell me?

CHRIS: Tell you what?

ANN: She says they think Joe is guilty.

CHRIS: What difference does it make what they think?

ANN: I don't care what they think, I just don't understand why you took the trouble to deny it. You said it was all forgotten.

CHRIS: I didn't want you to feel there was anything wrong in you coming here, that's all. I know a lot of people think my father was guilty, and I assumed there might be some question in your mind.

ANN: But I never once said I suspected him.

CHRIS: Nobody says it.

ANN: Chris, I know how much you love him, but it could never . . .

CHRIS: Do you think I could forgive him if he'd done that thing?

ANN: I'm not here out of a blue sky, Chris. I turned my back on my father, if there's anything wrong here now . . .

CHRIS: I know that, Ann.

ANN: George is coming from Dad, and I don't think it's with a blessing.

CHRIS: He's welcome here. You've got nothing to fear from George.

ANN: Tell me that . . . just tell me that.

CHRIS: The man is innocent, Ann. Remember he was falsely accused once and it put him through hell. How would you behave if you were faced with the same thing again? Annie, believe me, there's nothing wrong for you here, believe me, kid.

ANN: All right, Chris, all right. [*They embrace as* KELLER *appears quietly on porch.* ANN *simply studies him.*]

KELLER: Every time I come out here it looks like Playland! [*They break and laugh in embarrassment.*]

CHRIS: I thought you were going to shave?

KELLER [*sitting on bench*]: In a minute. I just woke up, I can't see nothin'.

ANN: You look shaved.

KELLER: Oh, no. [*Massages his jaw*] Gotta be extra special tonight. Big night, Annie. So how's it feel to be a married woman?

ANN [*laughs*]: I don't know, yet.

KELLER [*to* CHRIS]: What's the matter, you slippin'? [*He takes a little box of apples from under the bench as they talk.*]

CHRIS: The great roué!

KELLER: What is that, roué?

CHRIS: It's French.

KELLER: Don't talk dirty. [*They laugh.*]

CHRIS [*to Ann*]: You ever meet a bigger ignoramus?

KELLER: Well, somebody's got to make a living.

ANN [*as they laugh*]: That's telling him.

KELLER: I don't know, everybody's gettin' so Goddam edu-
cated in this country there'll be nobody to take away the garbage. [*They laugh.*] It's gettin' so the only dumb ones left are the
bosses.

ANN: You're not so dumb, Joe.

KELLER: I know, but you go into our plant, for instance. I got
so many lieutenants, majors, and colonels that I'm ashamed to ask
somebody to sweep the floor. I gotta be careful I'll insult somebody. No kiddin'. It's a tragedy: you stand on the street today and
spit, you're gonna hit a college man.

CHRIS: Well, don't spit.

KELLER [*breaks apple in half, passing it to* ANN *and* CHRIS]: I mean
to say, it's comin' to a pass. [*He takes a breath.*] I been thinkin',
Annie . . . your brother, George. I been thinkin' about your
brother George. When he comes I like you to *brooch* something
to him.

CHRIS: Broach.

KELLER: What's the matter with brooch?

CHRIS [*smiling*]: It's not English.

KELLER: When I went to night school it was brooch.

ANN [*laughing*]: Well, in day school it's broach.

KELLER: Don't surround me, will you? Seriously, Ann . . . You
say he's not well. George, I been thinkin', why should he knock
himself out in New York with that cut-throat competition, when
I got so many friends here; I'm very friendly with some big
lawyers in town. I could set George up here.

ANN: That's awfully nice of you, Joe.

KELLER: No, kid, it ain't nice of me. I want you to understand me. I'm thinking of Chris. [*Slight pause*] See . . . this is what I mean. You get older, you want to feel that you . . . accomplished something. My only accomplishment is my son. I ain't brainy. That's all I accomplished. Now, a year, eighteen months, your father'll be a free man. Who is he going to come to, Annie? His baby. You. He'll come, old, mad, into your house.

ANN: That can't matter any more, Joe.

KELLER: I don't want that hate to come between us. [*Gestures between* CHRIS *and himself*]

ANN: I can only tell you that that could never happen.

KELLER: You're in love now, Annie, but believe me, I'm older than you and I know—a daughter is a daughter, and a father is a father. And it could happen. [*He pauses.*] I like you and George to go to him in prison and tell him. . . . "Dad, Joe wants to bring you into the business when you get out."

ANN [*surprised, even shocked*]: You'd have him as a partner?

KELLER: No, no partner. A good job. [*Pause. He sees she is shocked, a little mystified. He gets up, speaks more nervously.*] I want him to know, Annie . . . while he's sitting there I want him to know that when he gets out he's got a place waitin' for him. It'll take his bitterness away. To know you got a place . . . it sweetens you.

ANN: Joe, you owe him nothing.

KELLER: I owe him a good kick in the teeth, but he's your father. . . .

CHRIS: Then kick him in the teeth! I don't want him in the plant, so that's that! You understand? And besides, don't talk about him like that. People misunderstand you!

KELLER: And I don't understand why she has to crucify the man.

CHRIS: Well, it's her father, if she feels . . .

KELLER: No, no. . . .

CHRIS [*almost angrily*]: What's it to you? Why . . . ?

KELLER [*a commanding outburst in his high nervousness*]: A father is a father! [*As though the outburst had revealed him, he looks about, wanting to retract it. His hand goes to his cheek.*] I better . . . I better shave. [*He turns and a smile is on his face. To* ANN] I didn't mean to yell at you, Annie.

ANN: Let's forget the whole thing, Joe.

KELLER: Right. [*To* CHRIS] She's likable.

CHRIS [*a little peeved at the man's stupidity*]: Shave, will you?

KELLER: Right again.

[*As he turns to porch* LYDIA *comes hurrying from her house,* R.]

LYDIA: I forgot all about it . . . [*Seeing* CHRIS *and* ANN] Hya. [*To* JOE] I promised to fix Kate's hair for tonight. Did she comb it yet?

KELLER: Always a smile, hey, Lydia?

LYDIA: Sure, why not?

KELLER [*going up on porch*]: Come on up and comb my Katie's hair. [LYDIA *goes up on porch.*] She's got a big night, make her beautiful.

LYDIA: I will.

KELLER [*he holds door open for her and she goes into kitchen. To* CHRIS *and* ANN]: Hey, that could be a song. [*He sings softly.*]

"Come on up and comb my Katie's hair . . .

Oh, come on up, 'cause she's my lady fair—"

[*To* ANN] How's that for one year of night school? [*He continues singing as he goes into kitchen.*]

"Oh, come on up, come on up, and comb my lady's hair——"

[JIM BAYLISS *rounds corner of driveway, walking rapidly.* JIM *crosses to* CHRIS, *motions him up and pulls him down to stage* L., *excitedly.* KELLER *stands just inside kitchen door, watching them.*]

CHRIS: What's the matter? Where is he?

JIM: Where's your mother?

CHRIS: Upstairs, dressing.

ANN [*crossing to them rapidly*]: What happened to George?

JIM: I asked him to wait in the car. Listen to me now. Can you take some advice? [*They wait.*] Don't bring him in here.

ANN: Why?

JIM: Kate is in bad shape, you can't explode this in front of her.

ANN: Explode what?

JIM: You know why he's here, don't try to kid it away. There's blood in his eye; drive him somewhere and talk to him alone.

[ANN *turns to go up drive, takes a couple of steps, sees* KELLER *and stops. He goes quietly on into house.*]

CHRIS [*shaken, and therefore angered*]: Don't be an old lady.

JIM: He's come to take her home. What does that mean? [*To* ANN] You know what that means. Fight it out with him someplace else.

ANN [*she comes back down toward* CHRIS]: I'll drive . . . him somewhere.

CHRIS [*goes to her*]: No.

JIM: Will you stop being an idiot?

CHRIS: Nobody's afraid of him here. Cut that out! [*He starts for driveway, but is brought up short by* GEORGE, *who enters there.* GEORGE *is Chris's age, but a paler man, now on the edge of his self-restraint. He speaks quietly, as though afraid to find himself screaming. An instant's hesitation and* CHRIS *steps up to him, hand extended, smiling.*] Helluva way to do; what're you sitting out there for?

GEORGE: Doctor said your mother isn't well, I . . .

CHRIS: So what? She'd want to see you, wouldn't she? We've been waiting for you all afternoon. [*He puts his hand on* GEORGE'S *arm, but* GEORGE *pulls away, coming across toward* ANN.]

ANN [*touching his collar*]: This is filthy, didn't you bring another shirt? [GEORGE *breaks away from her, and moves down and* L., *examining the yard. Door opens, and he turns rapidly, thinking it is Kate, but it's Sue. She looks at him, he turns away and moves on* L., *to fence. He looks over it at his former home.* SUE *comes downstage.*]

SUE [*annoyed*]: How about the beach, Jim?

JIM: Oh, it's too hot to drive.

SUE: How'd you get to the station—Zeppelin?

CHRIS: This is Mrs. Bayliss, George. [*Calling, as* GEORGE *pays no attention, staring at house off* L.] George! [GEORGE *turns.*] Mrs. Bayliss.

SUE: How do you do.

GEORGE [*removing his hat*]: You're the people who bought our house, aren't you?

SUE: That's right. Come and see what we did with it before you leave.

GEORGE [*he walks down and away from her*]: I liked it the way it was.

SUE [*after a brief pause*]: He's frank, isn't he?

JIM [*pulling her off* L.] See you later. . . . Take it easy, fella. [*They exit*, L.]

CHRIS [*calling after them*]: Thanks for driving him! [*Turning to George*] How about some grape juice? Mother made it especially for you.

GEORGE [*with forced appreciation*]: Good old Kate, remembered my grape juice.

CHRIS: You drank enough of it in this house. How've you been, George?—Sit down.

GEORGE [*he keeps moving*]: It takes me a minute. [*Looking around*] It seems impossible.

CHRIS: What?

GEORGE: I'm back here.

CHRIS: Say, you've gotten a little nervous, haven't you?

GEORGE: Yeah, toward the end of the day. What're you, big executive now?

CHRIS: Just kind of medium. How's the law?

GEORGE: I don't know. When I was studying in the hospital it seemed sensible, but outside there doesn't seem to be much of a law. The trees got thick, didn't they? [*Points to stump*] What's that?

CHRIS: Blew down last night. We had it there for Larry. You know.

GEORGE: Why, afraid you'll forget him?

CHRIS [*starts for George*]: Kind of a remark is that?

ANN [*breaking in, putting a restraining hand on* CHRIS]: When did you start wearing a hat?

GEORGE [*discovers hat in his hand*]: Today. From now on I decided to look like a lawyer, anyway. [*He holds it up to her.*] Don't you recognize it?

ANN: Why? Where . . . ?

GEORGE: Your father's . . . he asked me to wear it.

ANN: . . . How is he?

GEORGE: He got smaller.

ANN: Smaller?

GEORGE: Yeah, little. [*Holds out his hand to measure*] He's a little man. That's what happens to suckers, you know. It's good I went to him in time—another year there'd be nothing left but his smell.

CHRIS: What's the matter, George, what's the trouble?

GEORGE: The trouble? The trouble is when you make suckers out of people once, you shouldn't try to do it twice.

CHRIS: What does that mean?

GEORGE [*to* ANN]: You're not married yet, are you?

ANN: George, will you sit down and stop—?

GEORGE: Are you married yet?

ANN: No, I'm not married yet.

GEORGE: You're not going to marry him.

ANN: Why am I not going to marry him?

GEORGE: Because his father destroyed your family.

CHRIS: Now look, George . . .

GEORGE: Cut it short, Chris. Tell her to come home with me. Let's not argue, you know what I've got to say.

CHRIS: George, you don't want to be the voice of God, do you?

GEORGE: I'm . . .

CHRIS: That's been your trouble all your life, George, you dive into things. What kind of a statement is that to make? You're a big boy now.

GEORGE: I'm a big boy now.

CHRIS: Don't come bulling in here. If you've got something to say, be civilized about it.

GEORGE: Don't civilize me!

ANN: Shhh!

CHRIS [*ready to hit him*]: Are you going to talk like a grown man or aren't you?

ANN [*quickly, to forestall an outburst*]: Sit down, dear. Don't be angry, what's the matter? [*He allows her to seat him, looking at her.*] Now what happened? You kissed me when I left, now you . . .

GEORGE [*breathlessly*]: My life turned upside down since then. I couldn't go back to work when you left. I wanted to go to Dad and tell him you were going to be married. It seemed impossible not to tell him. He loved you so much . . . [*He pauses.*] Annie . . . we did a terrible thing. We can never be forgiven. Not even to send him a card at Christmas. I didn't see him once since I got home from the war! Annie, you don't know what was done to that man. You don't know what happened.

ANN [*afraid*]: Of course I know.

GEORGE: You can't know, you wouldn't be here. Dad came to work that day. The night foreman came to him and showed him the cylinder heads . . . they were coming out of the process with defects. There was something wrong with the process. So Dad went directly to the phone and called here and told Joe to come down right away. But the morning passed. No sign of Joe. So Dad called again. By this time he had over a hundred defectives. The Army was screaming for stuff and Dad didn't have anything to ship. So Joe told him . . . on the phone he told him to weld, cover up the cracks in any way he could, and ship them out.

CHRIS: Are you through now?

GEORGE [*surging up at him*]: I'm not through now! [*Back to* ANN] Dad was afraid. He wanted Joe there if he was going to do it. But Joe can't come down . . . he's sick. Sick! He suddenly gets the flu! Suddenly! But he promised to take responsibility. Do you understand what I'm saying? On the telephone you can't have responsibility! In a court you can always deny a phone call and that's exactly what he did. They knew he was a liar the first time, but in the appeal they believed that rotten lie and now Joe is a big shot and your father is the patsy. [*He gets up.*] Now what're you going to do? Eat his food, sleep in his bed? Answer me; what're you going to do?

CHRIS: What're you going to do, George?

GEORGE: He's too smart for me, I can't prove a phone call.

CHRIS: Then how dare you come in here with that rot?

ANN: George, the court . . .

GEORGE: The court didn't know your father! But you know him. You know in your heart Joe did it.

CHRIS [*whirling him around*]: Lower your voice or I'll throw you out of here!

GEORGE: She knows. She knows.

CHRIS [*to* ANN]: Get him out of here, Ann. Get him out of here.

ANN: George, I know everything you've said. Dad told that whole thing in court, and they . . .

GEORGE [*almost a scream*]: The court did not know him, Annie!

ANN: Shhh!—But he'll say anything, George. You know how quick he can lie.

GEORGE [*turning to* CHRIS, *with deliberation*]: I'll ask you something, and look me in the eye when you answer me.

CHRIS: I'll look you in the eye.

GEORGE: You know your father . . .

CHRIS: I know him well.

GEORGE: And he's the kind of boss to let a hundred and twenty-one cylinder heads be repaired and shipped out of his shop without even knowing about it?

CHRIS: He's that kind of boss.

GEORGE: And that's the same Joe Keller who never left his shop without first going around to see that all the lights were out.

CHRIS [*with growing anger*]: The same Joe Keller.

GEORGE: The same man who knows how many minutes a day his workers spend in the toilet.

CHRIS: The same man.

GEORGE: And my father, that frightened mouse who'd never buy a shirt without somebody along—that man would dare do such a thing on his own?

CHRIS: On his own. And because he's a frightened mouse this is another thing he'd do;—throw the blame on somebody else because he's not man enough to take it himself. He tried it in court but it didn't work, but with a fool like you it works!

GEORGE: Oh, Chris, you're a liar to yourself!

ANN [*deeply shaken*]: Don't talk like that!

CHRIS [*sits facing* GEORGE]: Tell me, George. What happened? The court record was good enough for you all these years, why isn't it good now? Why did you believe it all these years?

GEORGE [*after a slight pause*]: Because you believed it. . . . That's the truth, Chris. I believed everything, because I thought you did. But today I heard it from his mouth. From his mouth it's altogether different than the record. Anyone who knows him, and knows your father, will believe it from his mouth. Your Dad took everything we have. I can't beat that. But she's one item he's not going to grab. [*He turns to* ANN.] Get your things. Everything they have is covered with blood. You're not the kind of a girl who can live with that. Get your things.

CHRIS: Ann . . . you're not going to believe that, are you?

ANN [*she goes to him*]: You know it's not true, don't you?

GEORGE: How can he tell you? It's his father. [*To* CHRIS] None of these things ever even cross your mind?

CHRIS: Yes, they crossed my mind. Anything can cross your mind!

GEORGE: *He knows,* Annie. He knows!

CHRIS: The Voice of God!

GEORGE: Then why isn't your name on the business? Explain that to her!

CHRIS: What the hell has that got to do . . . ?

GEORGE: Annie, why isn't his name on it?

CHRIS: Even when I don't own it!

GEORGE: Who're you kidding? Who gets it when he dies? [*To* ANN] Open your eyes, you know the both of them, isn't that the first thing they'd do, the way they love each other?—J. O. Keller & Son? [*Pause.* ANN *looks from him to* CHRIS.] I'll settle it. Do you want to settle it, or are you afraid to?

CHRIS: . . . What do you mean?

GEORGE: Let me go up and talk to your father. In ten minutes you'll have the answer. Or are you afraid of the answer?

CHRIS: I'm not afraid of the answer. I know the answer. But my mother isn't well and I don't want a fight here now.

GEORGE: Let me go to him.

CHRIS: You're not going to start a fight here now.

GEORGE [*to* ANN]: What more do you want!!! [*There is a sound of footsteps in the house.*]

ANN [*turns her head suddenly toward house*]: Someone's coming.

CHRIS [*to* GEORGE, *quietly*]: You won't say anything now.

ANN: You'll go soon. I'll call a cab.

GEORGE: You're coming with me.

ANN: And don't mention marriage, because we haven't told her yet.

GEORGE: You're coming with me.

ANN: You understand? Don't . . . George, you're not going to start anything now! [*She hears footsteps.*] Shsh! [MOTHER *enters on porch. She is dressed almost formally, her hair is fixed. They are all turned toward her. On seeing* GEORGE *she raises both hands, comes down toward him.*]

MOTHER: Georgie, Georgie.

GEORGE [*he has always liked her*]: Hello, Kate.

MOTHER [*she cups his face in her hands*]: They made an old man out of you. [*Touches his hair*] Look, you're gray.

GEORGE [*her pity, open and unabashed, reaches into him, and he smiles sadly*]: I know, I . . .

MOTHER: I told you when you went away, don't try for medals.

GEORGE [*he laughs, tiredly*]: I didn't try, Kate. They made it very easy for me.

MOTHER [*actually angry*]: Go on. You're all alike. [*To* ANN] Look at him, why did you say he's fine? He looks like a ghost.

GEORGE [*relishing her solicitude*]: I feel all right.

MOTHER: I'm sick to look at you. What's the matter with your mother, why don't she feed you?

ANN: He just hasn't any appetite.

MOTHER: If he ate in my house he'd have an appetite. [*To* ANN] I pity your husband! [*To* GEORGE] Sit down. I'll make you a sandwich.

GEORGE [*sits with an embarrassed laugh*]: I'm really not hungry.

MOTHER: Honest to God, it breaks my heart to see what happened to all the children. How we worked and planned for you, and you end up no better than us.

GEORGE [*with deep feeling for her*]: You . . . you haven't changed at all, you know that, Kate?

MOTHER: None of us changed, Georgie. We all love you. Joe was just talking about the day you were born and the water got shut off. People were carrying basins from a block away—a stranger would have thought the whole neighborhood was on fire! [*They laugh. She sees the juice. To* ANN] Why didn't you give him some juice!

ANN [*defensively*]: I offered it to him.

MOTHER [*scoffingly*]: You offered it to him! [*Thrusting glass into* GEORGE's *hand*] Give it to him! [*To* GEORGE, *who is laughing*] And now you're going to sit here and drink some juice . . . and look like something!

GEORGE [*sitting*]: Kate, I feel hungry already.

CHRIS [*proudly*]: She could turn Mahatma Gandhi into a heavyweight!

MOTHER [*to* CHRIS, *with great energy*]: Listen, to hell with the restaurant! I got a ham in the icebox, and frozen strawberries, and avocados, and . . .

ANN: Swell, I'll help you!

GEORGE: The train leaves at eight-thirty, Ann.

MOTHER [*to* ANN]: You're leaving?

CHRIS: No, Mother, she's not . . .

ANN [*breaking through it, going to* GEORGE]: You hardly got here; give yourself a chance to get acquainted again.

CHRIS: Sure, you don't even know us any more.

MOTHER: Well, Chris, if they can't stay, don't . . .

CHRIS: No, it's just a question of George, Mother, he planned on . . .

GEORGE [*he gets up politely, nicely, for Kate's sake*]: Now wait a minute, Chris . . .

CHRIS [*smiling and full of command, cutting him off*]: If you want to go, I'll drive you to the station now, but if you're staying, no arguments while you're here.

MOTHER [*at last confessing the tension*]: Why should he argue? [*She goes to him, and with desperation and compassion, stroking his hair*] Georgie and us have no argument. How could we have an argument, Georgie? We all got hit by the same lightning, how can you . . . ? Did you see what happened to Larry's tree, Georgie? [*She has taken his arm, and unwillingly he moves across stage with her.*] Imagine? While I was dreaming of him in the middle of the night, the wind came along and . . . [LYDIA *enters on porch. As soon as she sees him.*]

LYDIA: Hey, Georgie! Georgie! Georgie! Georgie! Georgie! [*She comes down to him eagerly. She has a flowered hat in her hand, which Kate takes from her as she goes to* GEORGE.]

GEORGE [*they shake hands eagerly, warmly*]: Hello, Laughy. What'd you do, grow?

LYDIA: I'm a big girl now.

MOTHER [*taking hat from her*]: Look what she can do to a hat!

ANN [*to* LYDIA, *admiring the hat*]: Did you make that?

MOTHER: In ten minutes! [*She puts it on.*]

LYDIA [*fixing it on her head*]: I only rearranged it.

GEORGE: You still make your own clothes?

CHRIS [*of* MOTHER]: Ain't she classy! All she needs now is a Russian wolfhound.

MOTHER [*moving her head from* L. *to* R.]: It feels like somebody is sitting on my head.

ANN: No, it's beautiful, Kate.

MOTHER [*kisses* LYDIA—*to* GEORGE]: She's a genius! You should've married her. [*They laugh.*] This one can feed you!

LYDIA [*strangely embarrassed*]: Oh, stop that, Kate.

GEORGE [*to* LYDIA]: Didn't I hear you had a baby?

MOTHER: You don't hear so good. She's got three babies.

GEORGE [*a little hurt by it—to* LYDIA]: No kidding, three?

LYDIA: Yeah, it was one, two, three—You've been away a long time, Georgie.

GEORGE: I'm beginning to realize.

MOTHER [*to* CHRIS *and* GEORGE]: The trouble with you kids is you *think* too much.

LYDIA: Well, we think, too.

MOTHER: Yes, but not all the time.

GEORGE [*with almost obvious envy*]: They never took Frank, heh?

LYDIA [*a little apologetically*]: No, he was always one year ahead of the draft.

MOTHER: It's amazing. When they were calling boys twenty-seven Frank was just twenty-eight, when they made it twenty-eight he was just twenty-nine. That's why he took up astrology. It's all in when you were born, it just goes to show.

CHRIS: What does it go to show?

MOTHER [*to* CHRIS]: Don't be so intelligent. Some superstitions are very nice! [*To* LYDIA] Did he finish Larry's horoscope?

LYDIA: I'll ask him now, I'm going in. [*To* GEORGE, *a little sadly, almost embarrassed*] Would you like to see my babies? Come on.

GEORGE: I don't think so, Lydia.

LYDIA [*understanding*]: All right. Good luck to you, George.

GEORGE: Thanks. And to you . . . And Frank. [*She smiles at him, turns and goes off* R. *to her house.* GEORGE *stands staring after her.*]

LYDIA [*as she runs off*]: Oh, Frank!

MOTHER [*reading his thoughts*]: She got pretty, heh?

GEORGE [*sadly*]: Very pretty.

MOTHER [*as a reprimand*]: She's beautiful, you damned fool!

GEORGE [*looks around longingly; and softly, with a catch in his throat*]: She makes it seem so nice around here.

MOTHER [*shaking her finger at him*]: Look what happened to you because you wouldn't listen to me! I told you to marry that girl and stay out of the war!

GEORGE [*laughs at himself*]: She used to laugh too much.

MOTHER: And you didn't laugh enough. While you were getting mad about Fascism Frank was getting into her bed.

GEORGE [*to* CHRIS]: He won the war, Frank.

CHRIS: All the battles.

MOTHER [*in pursuit of this mood*]: The day they started the draft, Georgie, I told you you loved that girl.

CHRIS [*laughs*]: And truer love hath no man!

MOTHER: I'm smarter than any of you.

GEORGE [*laughing*]: She's wonderful!

MOTHER: And now you're going to listen to me, George. You had big principles, Eagle Scouts the three of you; so now I got a tree, and this one, [*Indicating* CHRIS] when the weather gets bad he can't stand on his feet; and that big dope [*Pointing to* LYDIA'S *house*] next door who never reads anything but Andy Gump has three children and his house paid off. Stop being a philosopher, and look after yourself. Like Joe was just saying—you move back here, he'll help you get set, and I'll find you a girl and put a smile on your face.

GEORGE: Joe? Joe wants me here?

ANN [*eagerly*]: He asked me to tell you, and I think it's a good idea.

MOTHER: Certainly. Why must you make believe you hate us? Is that another principle?—that you have to hate us? You don't hate us, George, I know you, you can't fool me, I diapered you. [*Suddenly to* ANN] You remember Mr. Marcy's daughter?

ANN [*laughing, to* GEORGE]: She's got you hooked already!
[GEORGE *laughs, is excited.*]

MOTHER: You look her over, George; you'll see she's the most
beautiful . . .

CHRIS: She's got warts, George.

MOTHER [*to* CHRIS]: She hasn't got warts! [*To* GEORGE] So the
girl has a little beauty mark on her chin . . .

CHRIS: And two on her nose.

MOTHER: You remember. Her father's the retired police in-
spector.

CHRIS: Sergeant, George.

MOTHER: He's a very kind man!

CHRIS: He looks like a gorilla.

MOTHER [*to* GEORGE]: He never shot anybody. [*They all burst
out laughing, as* KELLER *appears in doorway.* GEORGE *rises abruptly,
stares at* KELLER, *who comes rapidly down to him.*]

KELLER [*the laughter stops. With strained joviality*]: Well! Look
who's here! [*Extending his hand*] Georgie, good to see ya.

GEORGE [*shakes hands—somberly*]: How're you, Joe?

KELLER: So-so. Gettin' old. You comin' out to dinner with us?

GEORGE: No, got to be back in New York.

ANN: I'll call a cab for you. [*She goes up into the house.*]

KELLER: Too bad you can't stay, George. Sit down. [*To*
MOTHER] He looks fine.

MOTHER: He looks terrible.

KELLER: That's what I said, you look terrible, George. [*They
laugh.*] I wear the pants and she beats me with the belt.

GEORGE: I saw your factory on the way from the station. It
looks like General Motors.

KELLER: I wish it was General Motors, but it ain't. Sit down,
George. Sit down. [*Takes cigar out of his pocket*] So you finally went
to see your father, I hear?

GEORGE: Yes, this morning. What kind of stuff do you
make now?

KELLER: Oh, little of everything. Pressure cookers, an assembly for washing machines. Got a nice, flexible plant now. So how'd you find Dad? Feel all right?

GEORGE [*searching* KELLER, *he speaks indecisively*]: No, he's not well, Joe.

KELLER [*lighting his cigar*]: Not his heart again, is it?

GEORGE: It's everything, Joe. It's his soul.

KELLER [*blowing out smoke*]: Uh huh—

CHRIS: How about seeing what they did with your house?

KELLER: Leave him be.

GEORGE [*to* CHRIS, *indicating* KELLER]: I'd like to talk to him.

KELLER: Sure, he just got here. That's the way they do, George. A little man makes a mistake and they hang him by the thumbs; the big ones become ambassadors. I wish you'd-a told me you were going to see Dad.

GEORGE [*studying him*]: I didn't know you were interested.

KELLER: In a way, I am. I would like him to know, George, that as far as I'm concerned, any time he wants, he's got a place with me. I would like him to know that.

GEORGE: He hates your guts, Joe. Don't you know that?

KELLER: I imagined it. But that can change, too.

MOTHER: Steve was never like that.

GEORGE: He's like that now. He'd like to take every man who made money in the war and put him up against a wall.

CHRIS: He'll need a lot of bullets.

GEORGE: And he'd better not get any.

KELLER: That's a sad thing to hear.

GEORGE [*with bitterness dominant*]: Why? What'd you expect him to think of you?

KELLER [*the force of his nature rising, but under control*]: I'm sad to see he hasn't changed. As long as I know him, twenty-five years, the man never learned how to take the blame. You know that, George.

GEORGE [*he does*]: Well, I . . .

KELLER: But you do know it. Because the way you come in here you don't look like you remember it. I mean like in 1937 when we had the shop on Flood Street. And he damn near blew us all up with that heater he left burning for two days without water. He wouldn't admit that was his fault, either. I had to fire a mechanic to save his face. You remember that.

GEORGE: Yes, but . . .

KELLER: I'm just mentioning it, George. Because this is just another one of a lot of things. Like when he gave Frank that money to invest in oil stock.

GEORGE [*distressed*]: I know that, I . . .

KELLER [*driving in, but restrained*]: But it's good to remember those things, kid. The way he cursed Frank because the stock went down. Was that Frank's fault? To listen to him Frank was a swindler. And all the man did was give him a bad tip.

GEORGE [*gets up, moves away*]: I know those things . . .

KELLER: Then remember them, remember them. [ANN *comes out of house.*] There are certain men in the world who rather see everybody hung before they'll take blame. You understand me, George? [*They stand facing each other,* GEORGE *trying to judge him.*]

ANN [*coming downstage*]: The cab's on its way. Would you like to wash?

MOTHER [*with the thrust of hope*]: Why must he go? Make the midnight, George.

KELLER: Sure, you'll have dinner with us!

ANN: How about it? Why not? We're eating at the lake, we could have a swell time.

GEORGE [*long pause, as he looks at* ANN, CHRIS, KELLER, *then back to her*]: All right.

MOTHER: Now you're talking.

CHRIS: I've got a shirt that'll go right with that suit.

MOTHER: Size fifteen and a half, right, George?

GEORGE: Is Lydia . . . ? I mean—Frank and Lydia coming?

MOTHER: I'll get you a date that'll make her look like a . . . [*She starts upstage.*]

GEORGE [*laughs*]: No, I don't want a date.

CHRIS: I know somebody just for you! Charlotte Tanner! [*He starts for the house.*]

KELLER: Call Charlotte, that's right.

MOTHER: Sure, call her up. [CHRIS *goes into house.*]

ANN: You go up and pick out a shirt and tie.

GEORGE [*he stops, looks around at them and the place*]: I never felt at home anywhere but here. I feel so . . . [*He nearly laughs, and turns away from them.*] Kate, you look so young, you know? You didn't change at all. It . . . rings an old bell. [*Turns to* KELLER] You too, Joe, you're amazingly the same. The whole atmosphere is.

KELLER: Say, I ain't got time to get sick.

MOTHER: He hasn't been laid up in fifteen years. . . .

KELLER: Except my flu during the war.

MOTHER: Huhh?

KELLER: My flu, when I was sick during . . . the war.

MOTHER: Well, sure . . . [*To* GEORGE] I meant except for that flu. [GEORGE *stands perfectly still.*] Well, it slipped my mind, don't look at me that way. He wanted to go to the shop but he couldn't lift himself off the bed. I thought he had pneumonia.

GEORGE: Why did you say he's never . . . ?

KELLER: I know how you feel, kid, I'll never forgive myself. If I could've gone in that day I'd never allow Dad to touch those heads.

GEORGE: She said you've never been sick.

MOTHER: I said he was sick, George.

GEORGE [*going to* ANN]: Ann, didn't you hear her say . . . ?

MOTHER: Do you remember every time you were sick?

GEORGE: I'd remember pneumonia. Especially if I got it just the day my partner was going to patch up cylinder heads . . . What happened that day, Joe?

FRANK [*enters briskly from driveway, holding Larry's horoscope in his hand. He comes to* KATE]: Kate! Kate!

MOTHER: Frank, did you see George?

FRANK [*extending his hand*]: Lydia told me, I'm glad to . . . you'll have to pardon me. [*Pulling* MOTHER *over* R.] I've got something amazing for you, Kate, I finished Larry's horoscope.

MOTHER: You'd be interested in this, George. It's wonderful the way he can understand the . . .

CHRIS [*entering from house*]: George, the girl's on the phone . . .

MOTHER [*desperately*]: He finished Larry's horoscope!

CHRIS: Frank, can't you pick a better time than this?

FRANK: The greatest men who ever lived believed in the stars!

CHRIS: Stop filling her head with that junk!

FRANK: Is it junk to feel that there's a greater power than ourselves? I've studied the stars of his life! I won't argue with you, I'm telling you. Somewhere in this world your brother is alive!

MOTHER [*instantly to* CHRIS]: Why isn't it possible?

CHRIS: Because it's insane.

FRANK: Just a minute now. I'll tell you something and you can do as you please. Just let me say it. He was supposed to have died on November twenty-fifth. But November twenty-fifth was his favorable day.

CHRIS: Mother!

MOTHER: Listen to him!

FRANK: It was a day when everything good was shining on him, the kind of day he should've married on. You can laugh at a lot of it, I can understand you laughing. But the odds are a million to one that a man won't die on his favorable day. That's known, that's known, Chris!

MOTHER: Why isn't it possible, why isn't it possible, Chris!

GEORGE [*to* ANN]: Don't you understand what she's saying? She just told you to go. What are you waiting for now?

CHRIS: Nobody can tell her to go. [*A car horn is heard.*]

MOTHER [*to* FRANK]: Thank you, darling, for your trouble. Will you tell him to wait, Frank?

FRANK [as he goes]: Sure thing.

MOTHER [calling out]: They'll be right out, driver!

CHRIS: She's not leaving, Mother.

GEORGE: You heard her say it, he's never been sick!

MOTHER: He misunderstood me, Chris! [CHRIS looks at her, struck.]

GEORGE [to ANN]: He simply told your father to kill pilots, and covered himself in bed!

CHRIS: You'd better answer him, Annie. Answer him.

MOTHER: I packed your bag, darling . . .

CHRIS: What?

MOTHER: I packed your bag. All you've got to do is close it.

ANN: I'm not closing anything. He asked me here and I'm staying till he tells me to go. [To GEORGE] Till Chris tells me!

CHRIS: That's all! Now get out of here, George!

MOTHER [to CHRIS]: But if that's how he feels . . .

CHRIS: That's all, nothing more till Christ comes, about the case or Larry as long as I'm here! [To GEORGE] Now get out of here, George!

GEORGE [to ANN]: You tell me. I want to hear you tell me.

ANN: Go, George! [They disappear up the driveway, ANN saying "Don't take it that way, Georgie! Please don't take it that way."]

[CHRIS turns to his mother.]

CHRIS: What do you mean, you packed her bag? How dare you pack her bag?

MOTHER: Chris . . .

CHRIS: How dare you pack her bag?

MOTHER: She doesn't belong here.

CHRIS: Then I don't belong here.

MOTHER: She's Larry's girl.

CHRIS: And I'm his brother and he's dead, and I'm marrying his girl.

MOTHER: Never, never in this world!

KELLER: You lost your mind?

MOTHER: You have nothing to say!

KELLER [*cruelly*]: I got plenty to say. Three and a half years you been talking like a maniac—

MOTHER [*she smashes him across the face*]: Nothing. You have nothing to say. Now I say. He's coming back, and everybody has got to wait.

CHRIS: Mother, Mother . . .

MOTHER: Wait, wait . . .

CHRIS: How long? How long?

MOTHER [*rolling out of her*]: Till he comes; forever and ever till he comes!

CHRIS [*as an ultimatum*]: Mother, I'm going ahead with it.

MOTHER: Chris, I've never said no to you in my life, now I say no!

CHRIS: You'll never let him go till I do it.

MOTHER: I'll never let him go and you'll never let him go . . . !

CHRIS: I've let him go. I've let him go a long . . .

MOTHER [*with no less force, but turning from him*]: Then let your father go. [*Pause.* CHRIS *stands transfixed.*]

KELLER: She's out of her mind.

MOTHER: Altogether! [*To* CHRIS, *but not facing them*] Your brother's alive, darling, because if he's dead, your father killed him. Do you understand me now? As long as you live, that boy is alive. God does not let a son be killed by his father. Now you see, don't you? Now you see. [*Beyond control, she hurries up and into house.*]

KELLER [CHRIS *has not moved. He speaks insinuatingly, questioningly*]: She's out of her mind.

CHRIS [*a broken whisper*]: Then . . . you did it?

KELLER [*the beginning of plea in his voice*]: He never flew a P-40—

CHRIS [*struck. Deadly*]: But the others.

KELLER [*insistently*]: She's out of her mind. [*He takes a step toward* CHRIS, *pleadingly.*]

CHRIS [*unyielding*]: Dad . . . you did it?

KELLER: He never flew a P-40, what's the matter with you?

CHRIS [*still asking, and saying*]: Then you did it. To the others.
[*Both hold their voices down.*]

KELLER [*afraid of him, his deadly insistence*]: What's the matter
with you? What the hell is the matter with you?

CHRIS [*quietly, incredibly*]: How could you do that? How?

KELLER: What's the matter with you!

CHRIS: Dad . . . Dad, you killed twenty-one men!

KELLER: What, killed?

CHRIS: You killed them, you murdered them.

KELLER [*as though throwing his whole nature open before* CHRIS]:
How could I kill anybody?

CHRIS: Dad! Dad!

KELLER [*trying to hush him*]: I didn't kill anybody!

CHRIS: Then explain it to me. What did you do? Explain it to
me or I'll tear you to pieces!

KELLER [*horrified at his overwhelming fury*]: Don't, Chris, don't . . .

CHRIS: I want to know what you did, now what did you do?
You had a hundred and twenty cracked engine-heads, now what
did you do?

KELLER: If you're going to hang me then I . . .

CHRIS: I'm listening, God Almighty, I'm listening!

KELLER [*their movements now are those of subtle pursuit and escape.*
KELLER *keeps a step out of* CHRIS'S *range as he talks*]: You're a boy,
what could I do! I'm in business, a man is in business; a hundred
and twenty cracked, you're out of business; you got a process, the
process don't work you're out of business; you don't know how
to operate, your stuff is no good; they close you up, they tear up
your contracts, what the hell's it to them? You lay forty years into
a business and they knock you out in five minutes, what could
do, let them take forty years, let them take my life away? [*His
cracking*] I never thought they'd install them. I swear to G
thought they'd stop 'em before anybody took off.

CHRIS: Then why'd you ship them out?

KELLER: By the time they could spot them I thought I'd have the process going again, and I could show them they needed me and they'd let it go by. But weeks passed and I got no kick-back, so I was going to tell them.

CHRIS: Then why didn't you tell them?

KELLER: It was too late. The paper, it was all over the front page, twenty-one went down, it was too late. They came with handcuffs into the shop, what could I do? [*He sits on bench at* C.] Chris . . . Chris, I did it for you, it was a chance and I took it for you. I'm sixty-one years old, when would I have another chance to make something for you? Sixty-one years old you don't get another chance, do ya?

CHRIS: You even knew they wouldn't hold up in the air.

KELLER: I didn't say that . . .

CHRIS: But you were going to warn them not to use them . . .

KELLER: But that don't mean . . .

CHRIS: It means you knew they'd crash.

KELLER: It don't mean that.

CHRIS: Then you *thought* they'd crash.

KELLER: I was afraid maybe . . .

CHRIS: You were afraid maybe! God in heaven, what kind of a man are you? Kids were hanging in the air by those heads. You knew that!

KELLER: For you, a business for you!

CHRIS [*with burning fury*]: For me! Where do you live, where ⌐u come from? For me!—I was dying every day and you ⌐ my boys and you did it for me? What the hell do you ⌐king of, the Goddam business? Is that as far as your ⌐ business? What is that, the world—the business? ⌐u mean, you did it for me? Don't you have a ⌐ live in the world? What the hell are you? ⌐nal, no animal kills his own, what are you? ⌐? I ought to tear the tongue out of your mouth, what must I do? [*With his fist he pounds down upon his father's shoulder. He stumbles away, covering his face as he weeps.*] What must I do, Jesus God, what must I do?

KELLER: Chris . . . My Chris . . .

CURTAIN

ACT THREE

Two o'clock the following morning, MOTHER *is discovered on the rise, rocking ceaselessly in a chair, staring at her thoughts. It is an intense, slight sort of rocking. A light shows from upstairs bedroom, lower floor windows being dark. The moon is strong and casts its bluish light.*

Presently JIM, *dressed in jacket and hat, appears from* L., *and seeing her, goes up beside her.*

JIM: Any news?

MOTHER: No news.

JIM [*gently*]: You can't sit up all night, dear, why don't you go to bed?

MOTHER: I'm waiting for Chris. Don't worry about me, Jim, I'm perfectly all right.

JIM: But it's almost two o'clock.

MOTHER: I can't sleep. [*Slight pause*] You had an emergency?

JIM [*tiredly*]: Somebody had a headache and thought he was dying. [*Slight pause*] Half of my patients are quite mad. Nobody realizes how many people are walking around loose, and they're cracked as coconuts. Money. Money-money-money-money. You say it long enough it doesn't mean anything. [*She smiles, makes a silent laugh.*] Oh, how I'd love to be around when that happens!

MOTHER [*shakes her head*]: You're so childish, Jim! Sometimes you are.

JIM [*looks at her a moment*]: Kate. [*Pause*] What happened?

KATE: I told you. He had an argument with Joe. Then he got in the car and drove away.

JIM: What kind of an argument?

MOTHER: An argument. Joe . . . he was crying like a child, before.

JIM: They argued about Ann?

MOTHER [*slight hesitation*]: No, not Ann. Imagine? [*Indicates lighted window above*] She hasn't come out of that room since he left. All night in that room.

JIM [*looks at window, then at her*]: What'd Joe do, tell him?

MOTHER [*she stops rocking*]: Tell him what?

JIM: Don't be afraid, Kate, I know. I've always known.

MOTHER: How?

JIM: It occurred to me a long time ago.

MOTHER: I always had the feeling that in the back of his head, Chris . . . almost knew. I didn't think it would be such a shock.

JIM [*gets up*]: Chris would never know how to live with a thing like that. It takes a certain talent . . . for lying. You have it, and I do. But not him.

MOTHER: What do you mean . . . he's not coming back?

JIM: Oh, no, he'll come back. We all come back, Kate. These private little revolutions always die. The compromise is always made. In a peculiar way. Frank is right—every man does have a star. The star of one's honesty. And you spend your life groping for it, but once it's out it never lights again. I don't think he went very far. He probably just wanted to be alone to watch his star go out.

MOTHER: Just as long as he comes back.

JIM: I wish he wouldn't, Kate. One year I simply took off, went to New Orleans; for two months I lived on bananas and milk, and studied a certain disease. It was beautiful. And then she came, and she cried. And I went back home with her. And now I live in the usual darkness; I can't find myself; it's even hard sometimes to remember the kind of man I wanted to be. I'm a good husband; Chris is a good son—he'll come back. [KELLER *comes out on porch in dressing-gown and slippers. He goes upstage—to alley.* JIM *goes to him.*]

JIM: I have a feeling he's in the park. I'll look around for him. Put her to bed, Joe; this is no good for what she's got. [JIM *exits up driveway.*]

KELLER [*coming down*]: What does he want here?

MOTHER: His friend is not home.

KELLER [*his voice is husky. Comes down to her*]: I don't like him mixing in so much.

MOTHER: It's too late, Joe. He knows.

KELLER [*apprehensively*]: How does he know?

MOTHER: He guessed a long time ago.

KELLER: I don't like that.

MOTHER [*laughs dangerously, quietly into the line*]: What you don't like . . .

KELLER: Yeah, what I don't like.

MOTHER: You can't bull yourself through this one, Joe, you better be smart now. This thing—this thing is not over yet.

KELLER [*indicating lighted window above*]: And what is she doing up there? She don't come out of the room.

MOTHER: I don't know, what is she doing? Sit down, stop being mad. You want to live? You better figure out your life.

KELLER: She don't know, does she?

MOTHER: She saw Chris storming out of here. It's one and one—she knows how to add.

KELLER: Maybe I ought to talk to her?

MOTHER: Don't ask me, Joe.

KELLER [*almost an outburst*]: Then who do I ask? But I don't think she'll do anything about it.

MOTHER: You're asking me again.

KELLER: I'm askin' you. What am I, a stranger? I thought I had a family here. What happened to my family?

MOTHER: You've got a family. I'm simply telling you that I have no strength to think any more.

KELLER: You have no strength. The minute there's trouble you have no strength.

MOTHER: Joe, you're doing the same thing again; all your life whenever there's trouble you yell at me and you think that settles it.

KELLER: Then what do I do? Tell me, talk to me, what do I do?

MOTHER: Joe . . . I've been thinking this way. If he comes back . . .

KELLER: What do you mean "if"? . . . he's comin' back!

MOTHER: I think if you sit him down and you . . . explain yourself. I mean you ought to make it clear to him that you know you did a terrible thing. [*Not looking into his eyes*] I mean if he saw that you realize what you did. You see?

KELLER: What ice does that cut?

MOTHER [*a little fearfully*]: I mean if you told him that you want to pay for what you did.

KELLER [*sensing . . . quietly*]: How can I pay?

MOTHER: Tell him . . . you're willing to go to prison. [*Pause.*]

KELLER [*struck, amazed*]: I'm willing to . . . ?

MOTHER [*quickly*]: You wouldn't go, he wouldn't ask you to go. But if you told him you wanted to, if he could feel that you wanted to pay, maybe he would forgive you.

KELLER: He would forgive me! For what?

MOTHER: Joe, you know what I mean.

KELLER: I don't know what you mean! You wanted money, so I made money. What must I be forgiven? You wanted money, didn't you?

MOTHER: I didn't want it that way.

KELLER: I didn't want it that way, either! What difference is it what you want? I spoiled the both of you. I should've put him out when he was ten like I was put out, and make him earn his keep. Then he'd know how a buck is made in this world.

Forgiven! I could live on a quarter a day myself, but I got a family so I . . .

MOTHER: Joe, Joe . . . it don't excuse it that you did it for the family.

KELLER: It's got to excuse it!

MOTHER: There's something bigger than the family to him.

KELLER: Nothin' is bigger!

MOTHER: There is to him.

KELLER: There's nothin' he could do that I wouldn't forgive. Because he's my son. Because I'm his father and he's my son.

MOTHER: Joe, I tell you . . .

KELLER: Nothin's bigger than that. And you're goin' to tell him, you understand? I'm his father and he's my son, and if there's something bigger than that I'll put a bullet in my head!

MOTHER: You stop that!

KELLER: You heard me. Now you know what to tell him. [*Pause. He moves from her—halts.*] But he wouldn't put me away though . . . He wouldn't do that . . . Would he?

MOTHER: He loved you, Joe, you broke his heart.

KELLER: But to put me away . . .

MOTHER: I don't know. I'm beginning to think we don't really know him. They say in the war he was such a killer. Here he was always afraid of mice. I don't know him. I don't know what he'll do.

KELLER: Goddam, if Larry was alive he wouldn't act like this. He understood the way the world is made. He listened to me. To him the world had a forty-foot front, it ended at the building line. This one, everything bothers him. You make a deal, overcharge two cents, and his hair falls out. He don't understand money. Too easy, it came too easy. Yes sir. Larry. That was a boy we lost. Larry. Larry. [*He slumps on chair in front of her.*] What am I gonna do, Kate . . .

MOTHER: Joe, Joe, please . . . you'll be all right, nothing is going to happen . . .

KELLER [*desperately, lost*]: For you, Kate, for both of you, that's all I ever lived for . . .

MOTHER: I know, darling, I know . . . [ANN *enters from house. They say nothing, waiting for her to speak.*]

ANN: Why do you stay up? I'll tell you when he comes.

KELLER [*rises, goes to her*]: You didn't eat supper, did you? [*To* MOTHER] Why don't you make her something?

MOTHER: Sure, I'll . . .

ANN: Never mind, Kate, I'm all right. [*They are unable to speak to each other.*] There's something I want to tell you. [*She starts, then halts.*] I'm not going to do anything about it. . . .

MOTHER: She's a good girl! [*To* KELLER] You see? She's a . . .

ANN: I'll do nothing about Joe, but you're going to do something for me. [*Directly to* MOTHER] You made Chris feel guilty with me. Whether you wanted to or not, you've crippled him in front of me. I'd like you to tell him that Larry is dead and that you know it. You understand me? I'm not going out of here alone. There's no life for me that way. I want you to set him free. And then I promise you, everything will end, and we'll go away, and that's all.

KELLER: You'll do that. You'll tell him.

ANN: I know what I'm asking, Kate. You had two sons. But you've only got one now.

KELLER: You'll tell him . . .

ANN: And you've got to say it to him so he knows you mean it.

MOTHER: My dear, if the boy was dead, it wouldn't depend on my words to make Chris know it. . . . The night he gets into your bed, his heart will dry up. Because he knows and you know. To his dying day he'll wait for his brother! No, my dear, no such thing. You're going in the morning, and you're going alone. That's your life, that's your lonely life. [*She goes to porch, and starts in.*]

ANN: Larry is dead, Kate.

MOTHER [*she stops*]: Don't speak to me.

ANN: I said he's dead. I know! He crashed off the coast of China November twenty-fifth! His engine didn't fail him. But he died. I know . . .

MOTHER: How did he die? You're lying to me. If you know, how did he die?

ANN: I loved him. You know I loved him. Would I have looked at anyone else if I wasn't sure? That's enough for you.

MOTHER [*moving on her*]: What's enough for me? What're you talking about? [*She grasps* ANN'S *wrists.*]

ANN: You're hurting my wrists.

MOTHER: What are you talking about! [*Pause. She stares at* ANN *a moment, then turns and goes to* KELLER.]

ANN: Joe, go in the house . . .

KELLER: Why should I . . .

ANN: Please go.

KELLER: Lemme know when he comes. [KELLER *goes into house.*]

MOTHER [*she sees Ann take a letter from her pocket*]: What's that?

ANN: Sit down . . . [MOTHER *moves* L. *to chair, but does not sit.*] First you've got to understand. When I came, I didn't have any idea that Joe . . . I had nothing against him or you. I came to get married. I hoped . . . So I didn't bring this to hurt you. I thought I'd show it to you only if there was no other way to settle Larry in your mind.

MOTHER: Larry? [*Snatches letter from* ANN'S *hand.*]

ANN: He wrote it to me just before he—[MOTHER *opens and begins to read letter.*] I'm not trying to hurt you, Kate. You're making me do this, now remember you're——Remember. I've been so lonely, Kate . . . I can't leave here alone again. [*A long, low moan comes from* MOTHER'S *throat as she reads.*] You made me show it to you. You wouldn't believe me. I told you a hundred times, why wouldn't you believe me!

MOTHER: Oh, my God . . .

ANN [*with pity and fear*]: Kate, please, please . . .

MOTHER: My God, my God . . .

ANN: Kate, dear, I'm so sorry . . . I'm so sorry. [CHRIS *enters from driveway. He seems exhausted.*]

CHRIS: What's the matter . . . ?

ANN: Where were you? . . . you're all perspired. [MOTHER *doesn't move.*] Where were you?

CHRIS: Just drove around a little. I thought you'd be gone.

ANN: Where do I go? I have nowhere to go.

CHRIS [*to* MOTHER]: Where's Dad?

ANN: Inside lying down.

CHRIS: Sit down, both of you. I'll say what there is to say.

MOTHER: I didn't hear the car . . .

CHRIS: I left it in the garage.

MOTHER: Jim is out looking for you.

CHRIS: Mother . . . I'm going away. There are a couple of firms in Cleveland, I think I can get a place. I mean, I'm going away for good. [*To* ANN *alone*] I know what you're thinking, Annie. It's true. I'm yellow. I was made yellow in this house because I suspected my father and I did nothing about it, but if I knew that night when I came home what I know now, he'd be in the district attorney's office by this time, and I'd have brought him there. Now if I look at him, all I'm able to do is cry.

MOTHER: What are you talking about? What else can you do?

CHRIS: I could jail him! I could jail him, if I were human any more. But I'm like everybody else now. I'm practical now. You made me practical.

MOTHER: But you have to be.

CHRIS: The cats in that alley are practical, the bums who ran away when we were fighting were practical. Only the dead ones weren't practical. But now I'm practical, and I spit on myself. I'm going away. I'm going now.

ANN [*goes up to stop him*]: I'm coming with you. . . .

CHRIS: No, Ann.

ANN: Chris, I don't ask you to do anything about Joe.

CHRIS: You do, you do . . .

ANN: I swear I never will.

CHRIS: In your heart you always will.

ANN: Then do what you have to do!

CHRIS: Do what? What is there to do? I've looked all night for a reason to make him suffer.

ANN: There's reason, there's reason!

CHRIS: What? Do I raise the dead when I put him behind bars? Then what'll I do it for? We used to shoot a man who acted like a dog, but honor was real there, you were protecting something. But here? This is the land of the great big dogs, you don't love a man here, you eat him! That's the principle; the only one we live by—it just happened to kill a few people this time, that's all. The world's that way, how can I take it out on him? What sense does that make? This is a zoo, a zoo!

ANN [to MOTHER]: You know what he's got to do! Tell him!

MOTHER: Let him go.

ANN: I won't let him go. You'll tell him what he's got to do . . .

MOTHER: Annie!

ANN: Then I will! [KELLER enters from house. CHRIS sees him, goes down R. near arbor.]

KELLER: What's the matter with you? I want to talk to you.

CHRIS: I've got nothing to say to you.

KELLER [taking his arm]: I want to talk to you!

CHRIS [pulling violently away from him]: Don't do that, Dad. I'm going to hurt you if you do that. There's nothing to say, so say it quick.

KELLER: Exactly what's the matter? What's the matter? You got too much money? Is that what bothers you?

CHRIS [with an edge of sarcasm]: It bothers me.

KELLER: If you can't get used to it, then throw it away. You hear me? Take every cent and give it to charity, throw it in the sewer. Does that settle it? In the sewer, that's all. You think I'm kidding? I'm tellin' you what to do, if it's dirty then burn it. It's your money, that's not my money. I'm a dead man, I'm an old

dead man, nothing's mine. Well, talk to me!—what do you want
to do!

CHRIS: It's not what I want to do. It's what you want to do.

KELLER: What should I want to do? [CHRIS *is silent.*] Jail? You
want me to go to jail? If you want me to go, say so! Is that where
I belong?—then tell me so! [*Slight pause*] What's the matter, why
can't you tell me? [*Furiously*] You say everything else to me, say
that! [*Slight pause*] I'll tell you why you can't say it. Because you
know I don't belong there. Because you know! [*With growing emphasis and passion, and a persistent tone of desperation*] Who worked
for nothin' in that war? When they work for nothin', I'll work for
nothin'. Did they ship a gun or a truck outa Detroit before they
got their price? Is that clean? It's dollars and cents, nickels and
dimes; war and peace, it's nickels and dimes, what's clean? Half
the Goddam country is gotta go if I go! That's why you can't
tell me.

CHRIS: That's exactly why.

KELLER: Then . . . why am *I* bad?

CHRIS: *I* know you're no worse than most men but I thought
you were better. I never saw you as a man. I saw you as my father.
[*Almost breaking*] I can't look at you this way, I can't look at myself! [*He turns away unable to face* KELLER. ANN *goes quickly to*
MOTHER, *takes letter from her and starts for* CHRIS. MOTHER *instantly
rushes to intercept her.*]

MOTHER: Give me that!

ANN: He's going to read it! [*She thrusts letter into* CHRIS'S *hand.*]
Larry. He wrote it to me the day he died. . . .

KELLER: Larry!?

MOTHER: Chris, it's not for you. [*He starts to read.*] Joe . . . go
away . . .

KELLER [*mystified, frightened*]: Why'd she say, Larry, what . . . ?

MOTHER [*she desperately pushes him toward alley, glancing at*
CHRIS]: Go to the street, Joe, go to the street! [*She comes down beside* KELLER.] Don't, Chris . . . [*Pleading from her whole soul*] Don't
tell him . . .

CHRIS [*quietly*]: Three and one half years . . . talking, talking. Now you tell me what you must do. . . . This is how he died, now tell me where you belong.

KELLER [*pleading*]: Chris, a man can't be a Jesus in this world!

CHRIS: I know all about the world. I know the whole crap story. Now listen to this, and tell me what a man's got to be! [*Reads*] "My dear Ann: . . ." You listening? He wrote this the day he died. Listen, don't cry . . . listen! "My dear Ann: It is impossible to put down the things I feel. But I've got to tell you something. Yesterday they flew in a load of papers from the States and I read about Dad and your father being convicted. I can't express myself. I can't tell you how I feel—I can't bear to live any more. Last night I circled the base for twenty minutes before I could bring myself in. How could he have done that? Every day three or four men never come back and he sits back there doing business. . . . I don't know how to tell you what I feel . . . I can't face anybody . . . I'm going out on a mission in a few minutes. They'll probably report me missing. If they do, I want you to know that you mustn't wait for me. I tell you, Ann, if I had him here now I could kill him—" [KELLER *grabs letter from* CHRIS'S *hand and reads it.*] [*After a long pause*] Now blame the world. Do you understand that letter?

KELLER [*he speaks almost inaudibly*]: I think I do. Get the car, I'll put on my jacket. [*He turns and starts slowly for the house.* MOTHER *rushes to intercept him.*]

MOTHER: Why are you going? You'll sleep, why are you going?

KELLER: I can't sleep here. I'll feel better if I go.

MOTHER: You're so foolish. Larry was your son too, wasn't he? You know he'd never tell you to do this.

KELLER [*looking at letter in his hand*]: Then what is this if it isn't telling me? Sure, he was my son. But I think to him they were all my sons. And I guess they were, I guess they were. I'll be right down. [*Exits into house.*]

MOTHER [*to* CHRIS, *with determination*]: You're not going to take him!

CHRIS: I'm taking him.

MOTHER: It's up to you, if you tell him to stay he'll stay. Go and tell him!

CHRIS: Nobody could stop him now.

MOTHER: You'll stop him! How long will he live in prison?— are you trying to kill him?

CHRIS [holding out letter]: I thought you read this!

MOTHER [of Larry, the letter]: The war is over! Didn't you hear?——it's over!

CHRIS: Then what was Larry to you? A stone that fell into the water? It's not enough for him to be sorry. Larry didn't kill himself to make you and Dad sorry.

MOTHER: What more can we be!

CHRIS: You can be better! Once and for all you can know there's a universe of people outside and you're responsible to it, and unless you know that you threw away your son because that's why he died.

[A shot is heard in the house. They stand frozen for a brief second.

CHRIS starts for porch, pauses at step, turns to ANN.]

CHRIS: Find Jim! [He goes on into the house and ANN runs up driveway. MOTHER stands alone, transfixed.]

MOTHER [softly, almost moaning]: Joe . . . Joe . . . Joe . . . Joe . . . [CHRIS comes out of house, down to MOTHER'S arms.]

CHRIS [almost crying]: Mother, I didn't mean to . . .

MOTHER: Don't, dear. Don't take it on yourself. Forget now. Live. [CHRIS stirs as if to answer.] Shhh . . . [She puts his arms down gently and moves towards porch.] Shhh . . . [As she reaches porch steps she begins sobbing, as]

THE CURTAIN FALLS

PROPERTY LIST

I

Garbage pail
Leaf burner
Sunday paper
Paper bag
Flower petals
Glass of water and aspirins
Ladder
Pot of raw stringbeans

II

Limb of broken-off tree
Tray with grape juice, pitcher, glasses
Scrap of paper
Hat (for George)
Flowered hat (for Lydia)
Sheet of paper
About 6 apples in small fruit box
Saw

III

Letter

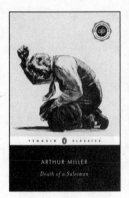

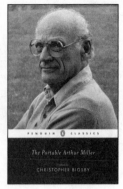

BY ARTHUR MILLER

DRAMA

After the Fall

All My Sons

Broken Glass

The Crucible

Death of a Salesman

An Enemy of the
People *(adaptation
of the play by Ibsen)*

Incident at Vichy

The Man Who Had
All the Luck

Mr. Peters'
Connections

DRAMA *continued*

The Price

Resurrection Blues

The Ride Down
Mt. Morgan

A View from the
Bridge

OTHER WORKS

Focus *(a novel)*

Echoes Down the
Corridor *(essays)*

Homely Girl, A Life
and Other Stories

Presence: Stories

Timebends
(autobiography)

COLLECTIONS

The Portable
Arthur Miller
*(edited by
Christopher Bigsby)*

VIKING CRITICAL
LIBRARY EDITIONS

Death of a Salesman
*(edited by
Gerald Weales)*

The Crucible *(edited
by Gerald Weales)*

PENGUIN
CLASSICS